INVADE THE MAN CAVE

Sports Secrets Guys Don't Share

by

Kate Delaney

TULLAMORE
PUBLISHING

Dallas, Texas

1ST EDITION

Interior design by Brian Moreland

Cover design by Brian Moreland

Cover photos:

© Dusty Cline - Fotolia.com

© Jason Stitt - Fotolia.com

© Pete Saloutos - Fotolia.com

© Yuri Arcurs - Fotolia.com

© Clarence Alford - Fotolia.com

© Paul Yates - Fotolia.com

© xymm - Fotolia.com

© Lovrencg - Fotolia.com

© Fxquadro - Fotolia.com

Printed in the U.S.A.

ISBN 978-1-5136-0381-0

To my mother, Kathleen Delaney,
for not only taking me to my first game but for also
teaching my brother Patrick and I that nothing is out of
reach if we play fair. She inspires me every day.

Acknowledgements

Thanks to my husband, Paul Joslin, for his countless words of encouragement and his gentle push to write this book. I also wish to thank Brian Moreland for his attention to detail on the book layout and design, along with polishing off the editing. Big thanks to Liz Lawless for encouraging me to write and stepping in to edit and promote the book. To Leann Garms for proofreading. The rest of the team at Build, Buzz, Launch: Lesley Lawless, Oscar Warren, TK Lawless, and Raul Enriquez for helping to get the word out.

Special thanks to my friend, Annie Zidarevich, for helping me navigate the world of sports and broadcasting and sitting through hours of tennis, both at the U.S. Open Tennis in New York and at Indian Wells in Palm Springs, California over the years. Special recognition goes out to my friend, Kris O'Donnell, for her unending support throughout the years. And thanks to Matt Johnson and Donovan

Madsen for incredible technical support.

Thanks to everybody who helped me in my sports career, especially Roger and Rick Blamire for putting me on this crazy path.

Thanks to my family for being there: Nancy Fitzgerald, the best aunt ever, Patrick and Crissy Delaney, Owen Delaney—artist extraordinaire—Harry Reynolds, the Lorincz family, the Goldstein family, especially Griffin and Pat Wardlow. Also Anne Marie Scola and Robin Fairbanks. Mika Teachout and Mimi Andrews, for their wicked brainstorming session.

To the ladies of the dog park for their friendship: Stacy Latamore, Johanna Hinkle, Jalynn Frey, Annie Dutton and Gail Wheeler.

Also, thanks to countless athletes, owners, managers, sports writers and others in the world of sports too numerous to mention who have joined me for interviews throughout the years, giving me material for many books in the years to come.

Contents

Part Six - Golf: PGA/LPGA and the Old Guys

Part Seven - College Football

Part Eight - College Hoops

Part Nine - Left Turns: Auto Racing

Part Ten - Tennis: Big Gamers

Part Eleven - Sports of All Sorts

Part Twelve - Rock Stars of Sports

Introduction

In putting this book together, I realized just how big of an influence sports has been in my life. Before any of the sports talk shows, I was always a fan of sports across the board. Growing up in New Jersey, just a stone's throw from Philadelphia, my mother took us to countless Flyers and Phillies games throughout the years, giving me endless hours of enjoyment. I know many reading this can relate to some of the experiences. Perhaps for some, you'll find a fact or two that takes you by surprise. I know in doing my research for the "Sports Shorts" radio segments, I have often been stunned by new things I learned. I hope you enjoy this little slice of my world.

Kate Delaney

PART ONE

National Football League

1

Leather Helmets
and Beyond

What would life be like without football in the United States? Unimaginable! The landscape is littered with people playing the great game somewhere every five minutes, or so I've been told. I mean all forms of football from a game of touch, or black-top to Pee Wee, high school, college, and on up to the pros. Your *Madden NFL* video game doesn't count!

My cousin Kevin is the Director of Athletic Communications at Rutgers, and he'd tell you that the first football game was played on a football field at the University. On Nov. 6, 1869, Rutgers beat the College of New Jersey, now known as Princeton. The final score, 6-4, seems a little more like a Rugby score and the game was very similar. The two teams played with a round ball just like soccer on a field that was 120 yards long and 75 yards wide. So how 'bout that? Jersey, the butt of countless jokes for various reasons we won't get into here, gave birth to the great game of football. Much more on college football in Part Seven of the book, including the all-time rabid fans!

Professional football truly became a reality in 1920 with the start of the American Professional Football League made up of 11 teams in Canton, Ohio. The deal was signed at a local car dealership. Football great Jim Thorpe was the original President. All the teams were from the Midwest including: the Akron Pros, Canton Bulldogs, Decatur Staleys, and the Buffalo All-Americans. I mentioned those teams because they seemed to be the most reliable; the league really had teams dropping out all the time. Usually, one team would pick another, sign a deal and play each other throughout the year.

Two years later the APFL was renamed the National Football League and now there were more teams. In fact by the mid '20s there were close to 25 teams. Chicago ended up with a team when George Halas, a player for the Decatur Staleys, bought the team for $100, moved it to the Windy City, and the Bears were born in 1922. In the early days there was even a scandal involving stacking a team with high school players to ensure that Chicago would end up with a winning record at the end of the season.

At the end of the 1932 season, the Chicago Bears and the Portsmouth Spartans finished tied for the best records in the league. The Bears were normally an outdoor team, but because the weather was so brutal, the NFL voted to hold a playoff game indoors at Chicago Stadium. Highly unusual, but dubbed as the first indoor American football game. People showed up in droves to watch and the playoff system was born. The League split into two divisions the following season and even held a championship game.

The early days with rule changes, better equipment, the introduction of an NFL Draft for college players, appointment of a Commissioner, and a Players Association—all of this and more laid the ground work for what the NFL has become in the modern era.

Today, there are 32 teams in two divisions: the American Football Conference and the National Football Conference. Both conferences are split into four divisions. Pro football season starts the Thursday after Labor Day, and the regular season usually finishes at the end of December. The goal is to get to the playoffs. It's a single elimination roller coaster ride that ends with two teams fighting to claim the Lombardi Trophy as the NFL Champ for the season.

There is no Championship Game bigger than the Super Bowl and there is nothing like being a part of that rich history. I had the good fortune of traveling with the Dallas Cowboys in the late '90s. The team still had future Hall of Famers Troy Aikman, Emmitt Smith and Michael Irvin. All three had been a part of three championship teams at the time. The Cowboys beat Buffalo back to back in 1993 and '94 and beat the Steelers in '97, so they all had three rings. I traveled with and covered these guys, who were like rock stars, everywhere they traveled. It really hit me when I flew with them to Philadelphia, my home town. When we got off the buses and arrived at a downtown hotel, there were hundreds of people. I thought this was a convention crowd but boy was I wrong. These were Cowboys fans waiting to greet their heroes. Unfortunately for me, I had no idea that's what would happen as I had my poor mother picking me up in the lobby. I could see her bobbing up and down in the distance, waving and really struggling. She was a petite blonde being smothered by the crowd. Nate Newton looked at me and realized what was happening and jumped to the rescue. He grabbed my hand and parted the crowd like Moses and the Red sea.

Fans are great but one thing was clear: the Dallas Cowboys wanted to win another championship. As Emmitt said so many times, the rushing records are special but it was about the team and the need to get back to the Super Bowl. I have never met any athlete, for that matter, who cared more about individual records over winning a championship. Although players with big records get bigger contracts and individual records add up when it comes to getting into the Hall of Fame, they don't guarantee a trip to the Super Bowl. We'll get to some of the all-time superstars in the NFL in a later chapter.

As far as team records go in the Super Bowl category, the Steelers have won the most with six, while the Cowboys and San Francisco 49ers each have five. It's been tough for players and fans in Minnesota and Buffalo. Both teams have lost all four Super Bowls they've been to in their history.

The outcome of the season also plays a part in the future when the teams look to the NFL after the season has wrapped up. Once the Super Bowl is over, team owners and coaches start looking at future talent for their clubs. Every April college players with the hopes and dreams of making a team are either squashed or realized at the annual NFL Draft. Teams are ranked in inverse order based on how they finished the previous season. The team with the most losses picks first in all the rounds and the two teams in the Super Bowl pick last. Currently, the Draft features 7 rounds and 224 players are picked. It gets interesting when teams trade to move up or trade away draft picks for other players on a roster. The Draft can be unpredictable, making it a must-see for the diehard football fan.

2

The Whole Enchilada:
Super Bowl

You can't talk about any Super Bowl and not talk about what an event it is in our lives. And I'm not just talking about in the United States. I mean globally as well. I wonder if the former owner of the Kansas City Chiefs, the late Lamar Hunt, who wanted to see the American Football League play the National Football League for a World Championship, had any idea how big the game would become?

The first Super Bowl was played at the Los Angeles Memorial Stadium in 1967 with the Packers pounding Hunt's Chiefs 35-10. Here's the interesting part: the inaugural game was watched by 60 million people, shattering all kinds of records. Super Bowl XLIX, 49 years later in 2015, drew an average of 114.4 million viewers with Seattle trying to win back to back Super Bowls taking on the New England Patriots. In the end it, became the most watched event on television of all time.

That Super Bowl will go down in history as one of the best finishes of all time by the way. The Patriots rallied to take the lead 28-24 with two minutes left in the game. What happened next will be debated for a long time. The Seahawks had a chance to hoist the Lombardi trophy again. All they had to do was score with 26 second left on the clock and the ball on New England's one-yard line. Instead of trying to run the ball into the end zone using the best back in the NFL, Marshawn Lynch, Coach Pete Carroll decided to go for a pass play. Seattle quarterback Russell Wilson's pass was intercepted by Pats rookie receiver, Malcolm Butler, and New England won the Super Bowl. Tom Brady was named MVP and knotted his third Super Bowl victory.

Doesn't the Super Bowl seem like a national holiday in the United States? Even the name "Super Bowl" immediately conjures up images of games we all remember. How about the fact that Hunt coined the name "Super Bowl" after watching his kids play with a super ball. It's true!

How many times have you been asked this question; "What are you doing for Super Bowl Sunday?" Chances are you are going to a party or hosting one at your house. It is the second biggest day for food consumption in the country, and here's a hint—the biggest day involves a Turkey in November.

These guesstimates on the food factor will wow you: 15,000 tons of chips will be eaten on Super Bowl Sunday. Eight million pounds of guacamole get consumed and, no surprise, pizza is the food of choice at many household—30 million pizzas were supposedly ordered in 2015. On average, it's been estimated that $50 million dollars is spent on food in this country days before the game to get ready for the party. Is it any surprise that 6 percent of the working population in the U.S. calls in sick the Monday following the Super Bowl?

The Super Bowl means big bucks all around. With such a captive audience it translates to instant brand recognition for the companies who produce everything from Chips to Cars. Super Bowl XLIX had more than 60 commercials attached to it costing $4.5 million for a 30-second spot. You do the math.

Besides watching the commercials, the half-time show is one of the most talked about and anticipated things about the game. It used to just be marching bands but Michael Jackson's appearance in 1993 changed that forever. Lots of big names have performed from U2's emotional performance with Bono singing "Where the Streets Have No Name", while the names of the victims of 9/11 were scrolled on a screen in the background to Bruce Springsteen singing, "Born to Run". The performance talked about the most was 2004's Janet Jackson/Justin Timberlake's appearance. Who knew that was going to happen? If you missed it Timberlake tore off a piece of Jackson's top exposing her breast, leading to an FCC fine of $550,000 for indecency to CBS stations televising the game. To this day Timberlake says it was a wardrobe malfunction. The NFL was embarrassed as it was the story that wouldn't go away. It became fodder for radio and television talk shows around the country.

Hosting a Super Bowl can also mean big bucks for the city that gets the nod from the NFL's selection committee. Thousands of people make the trek to the game, filling up hotels and restaurants and spending lots of money. Miami has played host city 10 times, with New Orleans a close second grabbing 9 of them.

I have been to 15 Super Bowls and I have to say one of my favorites to cover was the Packers 35-21 win over the Patriots in 1997. It was easy to maneuver around the French Quarter, and the air was ripe with excitement over the possibility of a grinder of a game. One of my all-time favorite talk show guests played a big role in the Green Bay win, the late great defensive lineman, Reggie White. He set a Super Bowl record with three sacks, two of them back to back in the third quarter.

So far the game has never been played anywhere where there isn't an NFL team but that could change in the future, and it's already been hinted at by the league's commissioner Roger Goodell. He has said that Los Angeles with or without a team could host the 50th Super Bowl to commemorate the first one ever played. Also, the idea of London has been broached in the past as a city for a Super Bowl. Wembley Stadium has hosted several NFL games in the past. Imagine how tough tickets would be to get for either of those Super Bowls should it become a reality!

Invade the Man Cave Tip

The Super Bowl is the end of the line every February. Conveniently it's right before Valentine's Day. Big Super Bowl parties are kind of like great weddings. Everyone excitedly arrives and the ritual ensues. The main characters are dressed up and on the field and we are staring at a screen watching the performance. Let's be honest. Don't we always want to know who is coming to the nuptials, so we're prepared. It's the same for the NFL. Look up the quarterback, offense and defense of both teams so you know the seating chart. A little knowledge goes a long way. Just remember there is a hibernation period that follows the end of an NFL season.

3

Hall of Fame

The Pro Football Hall of Fame releases the list of the new crop of guys that made it to the Hall each year during Super Bowl week, and like clockwork arguments erupt as to who was left off and why someone was chosen. So far 267 players, coaches, and other contributors deemed worthy have been enshrined at the Hall in Canton, Ohio. Immortalizing the greats of the game in Canton makes sense since, as you learned in a previous chapter, the first league, the American Professional League, started in that Ohio city.

Would you believe that the Hall of Fame has only been open since 1963? The first group of 17 charter members included Harold "Red" Grange. Known as "the Galloping Ghost," Grange was tough as nails and proved it on the field as a half-back for the University of Illinois. In just 20 games, he ran for 3,362 yards and scored 31 touchdowns. After college, he played for the Chicago Bears, and people came out in droves to see him. Grange was the star in the Bears 19-7 win over the New York Giants at the Polo Grounds in New York in a huge game in 1925. More than 70,000 people came to watch Grange that day, and he didn't disappoint scoring on a 35-yard interception return. Sammy Baugh was also chosen for the Hall that first year. Baugh was not only a star quarterback for the Washington Redskins from 1937 to 1952, but he could also punt and played some defensive end. Baugh was a two-time, All-American at Texas Christian University.

Obviously, Grange and Baugh were superstars of their era and were shoe-ins for any football Hall of Fame, but what are the criteria to make it to Canton? To be eligible to be nominated, a player or coach has to be retired for at least five years. The future inductees to the Hall of Fame are picked by a 44-member committee. Mostly sportswriters make up the group and usually its beat writers for NFL cities. You'll love this part: there are also eleven at-large delegates, mostly from cities that lost NFL teams and might pick one up in the future, plus a writer from the Pro Football Writers Association. The PFWA changes out its voter every two years but all the other appointments are for life. Usually only if someone resigns, retires or dies do they give up the vote. So, this group will choose 15 nominees while a Senior Committee will add two finalists from a group of players or coaches in the past that will make a final ballot of 17.

As I mentioned earlier, the choices elicit a lot of reaction from passionate football fans across the country. It didn't matter if I was doing sports talk locally in Dallas or New York or even for the Fox Sports Radio Network. As soon as the list was released the phone lines exploded with opinions on who was robbed and who shouldn't have gotten into the Hall. I think everyone who's followed Pro football has a list of people who should be in the Hall.

It took forever but finally Charles Haley was elected into the HOF in 2015! In a 12-year career in the NFL, Charles Haley won five Super Bowl Rings, two with the San Francisco 49ers in the 1988 and 1989 seasons, and three with the Dallas Cowbcys in 1992, '93, and '95. He started off as an outside linebacker and eventually found a home at defensive end. Haley was the ultimate pass rusher and the stats don't lie. He ended up with 100.5 quarterback sacks. He did have a temper during his playing days and could be violent, and this is why many people felt that it took so long for Haley, who retired in 1996, to get voted into the HOF.

I remember having a conversation about the Hall of Fame with the great Joe Namath when I was at the Super Bowl doing a radio show. We talked about who gets in and who doesn't. A QB his whole life, Namath agreed with me on Haley, saying that anyone who can alter the formation at the line because of what a threat he was to quarterbacks and with that many Super Bowl rings should be in the Hall. Namath, as you might remember, famously guaranteed his Jets would beat the Baltimore Colts before Super Bowl III. They did 16-7. "Broadway Joe" was enshrined in the Hall with another famous QB, former Cowboy, Roger Staubach. He led his teams to two Super Bowl wins and set countless records.

I could fill up a book on Hall of Fame players and their accomplishments on the field, and I still wouldn't have enough pages. I checked with the Pro Football Hall of Fame in Canton on its own archives of records. They have 18 million pages of documents! One thing that won't change, no matter how many records are set and broken, is that the entrance for players and coaches into the Pro Football Hall of Fame is not guaranteed, and there will always be arguments on who should and shouldn't get a bust in Canton.

PART TWO

Major League Baseball

4

National Pastime

Do you remember watching your first baseball game? I do! I was five years old and it was the Mets hosting the Phillies at Shea Stadium. I cried because even though we lived in New York my Grandmother rooted for Philadelphia and I wanted her team to win. Through the years, long before I started hosting radio sports talk shows, I went to countless games. My family moved from Queens to South Jersey, so we went to Veterans Stadium. My favorite player was the third baseman for Philly, Mike Schmidt.

Schmidt might be one of the best all-time third basemen in the history of the sport. He was part of the 1980 World Series team and played with the Phillies until he retired in 1989, setting all kinds of records. Rooting for players and teams like I did as a kid is part of what makes baseball our national pastime.

You spend all season chasing the players' and the teams' stats hoping for the payoff at the end—the World Series.

At least one hundred years before Schmidt even picked up a baseball glove and bat the game started to attract attention. Baseball historians often refer to the late 1860s as the beginning of baseball, with leagues and formalized competition. The National Association of Professional Base Ball Players was the game's first governing body, and by 1867 about 400 clubs, mostly in the northern part of the country, seemed to thrive. The first professional team was the Cincinnati Red Stockings, and they played their first game in May of 1869, creaming the Great Westerners of Cincy, 45-9. The Red Stockings won 57 games and lost none in matches against other clubs. The Red Stockings also played more than 70 games with other teams around the country, including Boston and San Francisco.

Finding its footing in the early years was tough with all the different leagues, but the most dominant ones were in the big cities, especially New York. It makes sense because of the potential fan base and revenue pouring in that the owners attracted some of the best players; an argument that some people still make over small market teams versus the big ones. That fight won't be solved here or anytime soon in my opinion! Although I know quite a few fans pushing for some sort of salary cap like they have in the National Football League.

In the early 1900s, the most prominent leagues—the National League, the American League and the National Association of Professional Baseball League (the minor league)—signed a National Agreement. Here baseball players became, in a sense, commodities as the dollar amounts attached to players were regulated, starting with the newly formed minor leagues. This also created a feeder system to the Majors.

Pitchers like Walter Johnson and Cy Young dominated the era as you rarely saw a home run. Can you imagine? Young played for four different teams from the start of his career in 1890 till the end in 1911. He pitched 7,355 innings, a record that still stands, and won 511 games. There are a slew of other records illustrating Young's amazing pitching skills. The year after he died at 88 years old in 1955, the award for the best pitcher in baseball, the Cy Young Award, was established. Walter Johnson was a close second to Young on the mound, only Johnson spent his entire career with one team, the Washington Senators. "The Big Train," as he was frequently called, won 417 games and pitched 110 shutouts; nobody will ever touch that shutout record. Prolific hitter Ty Cobb described Johnson as "the most powerful arm ever turned loose in a ballpark."

Baseball without a doubt was earning its name as "the National Pastime" with superstars like the ones I've mentioned, and a plethora of others too numerous to list. It still all goes back to the pride the fans feel for their team and the players they cheer on each season. Millions of Americans will go to at least one game at a Major League Ballpark in their lifetime, and given the length of the season there are plenty of opportunities.

Currently, there are 30 teams that make up Major League Baseball. The clubs are divided into two leagues, the American and the National. Since 1994, both leagues have had three divisions. One thing unique to the league is that the American League has the designated hitter rule, meaning the pitcher won't bat and a player takes his place in the lineup, only hitting and not fielding. The National League doesn't have this rule. No other sport of any of the majors has any different rules for different parts of participating leagues. This is the rare exception.

Starting in April every team will play 162 regularly scheduled games all the way through the end of September. As former Texas Ranger, Will Clark, used to tell me, "There is no clock in baseball," and boy isn't that the truth? We live these days in an era of instant gratification; something that's not possible in the great game of baseball. This is an old chestnut but one that rings true today when playing or following baseball. It's a marathon not a sprint.

5

Spring Training

Once the season is over those of us who think of baseball as a religion are already making plans for the following spring. Yep, who doesn't want to head to Arizona or Florida to join the baseball party? If you're a fan this is, hands down, the best way to watch rookies and veterans prep for the season. And here's the best part: you get a front row seat. It all starts in mid-February when pitchers and catchers report first, giving them the needed reps. The rest of the team joins in a few weeks later.

Some of my best memories of the great game come from years of spending weeks in Spring Training, mostly in Florida but also Arizona. One year I came home with an accidental souvenir from being hit in the ankle by a line drive. It was my fault. I was on the field during some batting practice and having a conversation with the former first baseman of the Texas Rangers, Rafael Palmiero, and I had my back turned. Not a good idea!

So how did Spring Training come about? It all started in the early 1900s when Major League Baseball teams started having their players get ready for the season in warmer climates. It always ran from February to Opening Day, which usually falls around April 1st. Where the teams trained was kind of all over the map early on. For instance, the Cubs practiced in Florida and Los Angeles in the 1920s while the St. Louis Cardinals made Hot Springs, Arkansas their home. My favorite is the Pirates, lucky guys; they got to go to Honolulu!

There are a few more interesting stops to mention when talking about Spring Training. Ever wonder about the Latin explosion in baseball? It's no secret that some great players have come from Dominican Republic and Puerto Rico. A compelling reason is during the 1950s the Yankees took advantage of the weather there and trained in the D.R. and in Havana, Cuba. The other cross-town rivals in New York, the Brooklyn Dodgers, did the same, spending time on those islands in the late 1940s. That would have been a fun trip!

Some teams like the Philadelphia Phillies went to the Sunshine State and never looked back. And how about this one? All but six of today's major league teams have trained in Florida at some point in their history, giving birth to the Grapefruit League. Today, fifteen teams go to Florida and fifteen do their spring training in Arizona.

Here are the Grapefruit teams you can catch in Florida: Braves, Red Sox, Orioles, Tigers, Astros, Marlins, Twins, Mets, Yankees, Phillies, Pirates, Cardinals, Rays, Jays and the Nationals. As for the Cactus crowd in Arizona: Diamondbacks, Cubs, White Sox, Reds, Indians, Rockies, Royals, Angels, Dodgers, Brewers, A's, Padres, Giants, Mariners, and the Rangers.

Lots of people take advantage of spring training. And with the incredible access to your favorite teams, it's no surprise that, according to Major League Baseball, almost two million people took in a game or two in the Phoenix area for Spring Training in 2015. And that means big bucks for the businesses. The current estimate in Phoenix and surrounding cities combined is around $320 million a year, and remember this is for about six weeks. In Florida they are reporting similar numbers with attendance well over two million. Between the two combined, it was an all-time attendance record for Spring Training in 2015.

6

All-star History

If you are a baseball fan, at some point in your life you owe it to yourself to make the trip to the Baseball Hall of Fame in Cooperstown, New York. This is the Promised Land for baseball players of all eras, and the treasures inside span more than a century of the national pastime.

I still have to pinch myself when I think about doing a radio show from inside the museum for a few nights before Rangers Hall-of-Famer Nolan Ryan was inducted back in 1999. During his career Ryan pitched seven no-hitters and had 5,717 strike-outs. Both are Major League records. He is the only player in the Hall of Fame to pitch in four different decades; Ryan played the game for 27 years. While he played for several different teams, including the Astros, Angels, and Mets, he finished the last five seasons with Texas and opted to go in as a Ranger. Now the CEO and President of the Texas Rangers, Nolan Ryan went into the Hall on the first ballot with 98.9% of the vote.

Ryan, like many of the other players in the Hall, was elected by the Baseball Writers Association of America. These are writers who have covered baseball for at least 10 years. To be considered, a player has to have been retired for five years and have at least 10 years of Major League baseball experience. A final ballot that the writers will mark will include 25 to 40 candidates. Every writer can vote for up to 10 players. If the player is named on 75% of the ballots or more they are elected into the Hall of Fame. As you can imagine, fans don't often agree with the choices!

The other road to the Baseball Hall of Fame is through the main Veterans Committee, made up of living Hall-of-Famers whose careers began after 1943 or later. In a nutshell, if a player isn't elected by the BBWAA within 20 years after his retirement from baseball, the Veterans can vote him into the Hall. There are several other committees under the Veterans umbrella to elect other players and managers from different leagues and even umpires. Ultimately, as it was during their careers it is all about the numbers.

No matter how they arrive every inductee gets a bronze plaque in the Hall of Fame Gallery. As of

2015, there are 310 elected members; 215 are players with their likeness and accomplishments on the wall. Here are a couple of fun facts about the plaques: The late great Jim "Catfish" Hunter pitched during his 15-year career with both the Oakland A's and the New York Yankees. He won three World Series with the A's in 1972, '73, and '74. Later he won two with the Yankees in '77 and '78. Catfish, elected to the Hall of Fame in 1987, said he couldn't make up his mind as to what team he wanted on the hat on his plaque. He enjoyed playing for A's owner Charlie Finley and Yankee owner George Steinbrenner. Therefore his hat has no logo.

Hunter's teammate at both clubs Reggie Jackson, a.k.a. "Mr. October," went into the Hall in 1993 after a 21-year playing career. Jackson played for four teams, including Oakland and New York, where he was part of the same World Series teams as Hunter. Jackson finished his career with 584 home runs and 1,702 hits. One of his biggest highlights happened in Game 6 of the 1977 World Series. As a member of the Yankees squad he hit three consecutive home runs, pretty much sealing his path to the Hall. Jackson was a first ballot Hall-of-Famer, getting 93.6% of the vote. On his cap is the Yankees logo.

This might be my favorite story about the plaques and logos. Dave Winfield had a baseball career that stretched 22 years, and he finished with 3,110 hits. Winfield played for six different teams, but a big chunk of his career was spent with the Yankees even though his lone World Series was with the Toronto Blue Jays in 1992. Furious at Yanks owner George Steinbrenner, Winfield decided to go into the Hall as a Padre, shocking most New York fans. So his logo is that of San Diego's. He was inducted in 2001 with 84.5% of the vote and was a first ballot Hall-of-Famer.

The Hall of Fame houses the biggest collection of baseball memorabilia in the world, including balls, bats, photos, uniforms, and such that go back to early days of the game. The Hall was started by a local hotel owner in Cooperstown, Stephen Carlton Clark, who was desperate to bring tourists to the sleepy little town. It worked! The Hall of Fame was dedicated in June of 1939, and the first inductees included: Ty Cobb, Babe Ruth, Honus Wagner, Christy Mathewson, and Walter Johnson.

Invade the Man Cave Road Tip

Score huge points with your baseball fan man by suggesting a trip to Cooperstown, New York. Single? Also a great place for a girl's weekend, and it's less than 4 hours from NYC. The home of the Major League Baseball Hall of Fame is located in the land of idyllic bed-and-breakfast spots. Going to the HOF is like visiting a cool museum, only baseball's treasures replace the paintings and sculptures.

PART THREE

National Basketball League

7

Nothing But Net

Watching an NBA game today, would you have ever guessed that it all started on a YMCA court with a couple of peach baskets? Physical Education teacher James Naismith needed something to help the athletes who participated in track while they were stuck inside during the winter months in Springfield, Massachusetts. In 1891, the first game of basketball was played with a soccer ball. Players ran up and down the gym, from end to end, to get the ball into the baskets, often passing the ball up court to teammates. There was no such thing as dribbling the ball in this early game!

Naismith moved on to University of Kansas a few years later but kept the ball rolling by having the guys that he coached take on others from nearby YMCAs. Soon the game caught fire around the country. Most of the early teams were comprised of players from the YMCAs all over the country. The game expanded through word of mouth to other schools, colleges, and universities.

Fast forward to 1947 and now you have the formation of the National Basketball Association. It started with 17 teams, some still around today like the Knicks, Lakers, Warriors, and Pistons. Kids started to identify with the players right away, reading the box scores in the paper and listening to the play-by-play of the action on the radio. The Boston Celtics dominated the conversations in the late '50s, making history by winning eight championships in a row starting in the 1958-59 season with a team full of talented players coached by Red Auerbach. Players like Bill Russell, Bob Cousy, and John Havlicek made up the core of the Celtics; they were the heart and soul of that team. Their streak will probably never be broken by any professional sports team. We could take it a step further: Boston was so dominant that the team not only set the record for consecutive wins but also won the NBA title 11 out of 13 years, starting in 1959.

The NBA wasn't the only game in town. There was fierce competition from another league, the ABA or American Basketball Association, trying to sign the best players before the NBA. Sometimes the ABA had the edge because they were able to sign college undergrads. One of the biggest names to sign with the ABA was Julius Erving, a.k.a. "Dr. J." Luckily for fans of the NBA, it wouldn't be too long before he would play with the 76ers. By 1977, the ABA cut a deal with the NBA, adding four new teams to the league at the time and bringing the total to 22 franchises.

Now, with more stars and a few new changes in the game, people were really starting to watch professional basketball. Some historians credit the popularity to the addition of the three-point field. Already in the ABA, three-pointers really opened up the floor in the NBA. By the late '70s and early '80s, rivalries like the Lakers' Magic Johnson and the Celts' Larry Bird created huge excitement for basketball around the country and even in other countries.

Once Michael Jordan joined the league in 1984 with the Chicago Bulls it wouldn't be long before kids everywhere were thinking about nothing but net. Certainly, there had always been pickup games across the country but now you couldn't always get a court, and everyone wanted to "be like Mike." With so many eyes on the game and no end in sight to the amount of money people would pay for tickets, merchandise, and almost anything related to the NBA and its stars, lots of cities began looking for funding for NBA teams.

By now Jordan was one of the best players on the floor along with teammate Scottie Pippen. The toughest ticket to get in Chicago was a seat at the United Center. After winning the three NBA titles from '90-'93, the Bulls lost superstar Michael Jordan. He retired after saying he was burned out on the game and his celebrity status, plus he was dealing with the murder of his father James Jordan. The Bulls struggled without the greatest player to ever play the game on the floor. The team finished the '93-'94 season at 55-27, losing to the Knicks in the second round of the playoffs.

Meanwhile, Jordan decided to sign a minor league contract with the Chicago White Sox and played baseball for a season, but by March of 1995 he sent out a press release saying just this, "I'm back." The Bulls managed to make it into the semi-finals against Orlando but many basketball insiders thought Jordan just wasn't the same, losing to the Magic in six games.

The '95-'96 season was magical for the Bulls after adding rebounding and defensive specialist Dennis Rodman to the team. If there was any doubt about Jordan's commitment to the game he shut the doubters down quickly. Chicago went on to finish the season with 72 wins, the best regular season ever in NBA history. Jordan was averaging 30 points plus per game. He and Scottie Pippen had now won 4 titles together after beating Seattle in the Finals. The Bulls then promptly won the next two NBA titles for another three-peat!

Michael Jordan cemented his place in history with spectacular play. His fade-away jumper was spectacular, and with his tongue often hanging, it became his signature shot. Jordan was aggressive when driving to the basket, the king of drawing fouls and then executing at the foul line finishing with over 8,700 free-throw attempts. And boy was he competitive! Michael Jordan was going to make the basket no matter what. He was all about "Nothing but Net."

8

Playoff Greats

I suppose as with almost everything in this book we might all look at Playoff greats through the lens of our favorite teams. Although, I think there are some undeniable stand-outs in this category from a couple of different eras. Keep in mind once again that this is in no particular order for you sports fans who are sticklers about ranking games 1 through 10 and so on.

Since I spent lots of time in New York both off and on the air, I have to pay homage to the former Knicks great Willis Reed. In the middle of a back and forth series with the Lakers it all came down to a Game 7 at Madison Square Garden in 1970. Reed had pulled a thigh muscle during Game 5 of the series and now had to have several painkiller shots to help deaden what he was feeling. He wasn't on the floor for the pre-game warm-ups, but just before the game started Willis made it to the court, hoisting a few shots, and the crowd erupted. Reed and the Knicks blew out the Lakers. At the half New York was already leading 61-37. At the final buzzer it was a 113-99 win and first Championship title for the Knicks.

In 1998, Michael Jordan and the Bulls had a chance to ice Game 6 and the NBA Title with a win over the Utah Jazz. I was in a sports bar in Texas watching it with friends, and I hate to say we doubted Chicago. The consensus was that Utah would pull it out and force a Game 7. Boy were we wrong! Down by one point, Jordan stole the ball from Karl Malone with six seconds to go in the game. After a timeout, the Bulls in-bounded the ball to Jordan who hit a 20-foot jumper for the 87-86 win and Jordan's sixth title in eight years.

Lakers great Magic Johnson wasn't called "winning time" for nothing. He saved his best stuff for the playoffs and was part of five championship teams starting with his rookie season. The Lakers were headed back to Philly with a 3-2 lead in their battle with the Sixers in the 1980 Finals. Only, star center Kareem Abdul-Jabbar couldn't play with a horribly sprained ankle. Magic was moved to center and scored 42 points, grabbing 15 rebounds in a 123-107 Game 6 NBA title winning game.

When you talk about playoff greats, Magic

Johnson's nemesis would have to make any list—the Celts great Larry Bird. Bird, who played for Boston for 13 seasons, was hot right off the bat in the playoffs just like Johnson. In just his second season for the Celts he was a key part of a team that came back from a 3-1 deficit to beat Philadelphia in three games by just a handful of points. In the 1981 Finals, Boston knocked off the Rockets in six games. The young Bird who would go on to win three NBA titles was averaging 15.3 points and 15.3 rebounds a game in the playoffs.

The Rockets had one of the all-time best clutch basketball players—Robert Horry. His nickname "Big Shot Rob" was well deserved after back to back titles with the Houston Rockets in '94 and '95. He was so key that he went on to also win three titles with the Lakers and two with the Spurs. Horry is one of two players that can claim that kind of hardware with multiple teams. To me one of his biggest baskets was against the Sacramento Kings with the Lakers trailing 99-97 in Game 4 of the Western Conference Finals in 2002. Just 11 seconds were left in the game, and it looked like the Kings were going to win and go up 3-1 on Los Angeles. Kobe Bryant and Shaquille O'Neal missed back to back lay-ups, and the ball was knocked away, but it bounced to Horry who hit a three-pointer with time expiring. After winning their series against the Kings, the Lakers then swept the Nets 4-0 in the Finals. Sweet!

Kobe Bryant would have to make the list of the playoff greats. He is without a doubt one of the best guards still playing in the NBA today. He is the leading scorer in the Lakers history and ranks sixth in the playoffs of all time scorers in the NBA's history. He has five championship rings, being part of a three-peat in 2000, 2001, 2002 and back to back in 2009 and 2010. There are a lot of highlights to pick from in Bryant's reel. Here's a good one: as a rookie facing lots of criticism, he nailed a bunch of jumpers to help ice Game 4 of a Finals series against the Pacers in 2000. The Lakers beat Indiana 4-2 in the series, and while Shaquille O'Neill was the MVP averaging 38 points and 16 boards, Bryant was already part of the glue.

In 2011, the Dallas Mavericks were given a chance to get by the Lakers in the West. They did with a four-game sweep and went on to beat Miami in the Finals in six games. This has to go down in the history of the NBA as one of the closest Finals of all time. After losing the first game, the Mavericks roared back in the second, down from 15 points in the 4th quarter, winning it on a driving left-handed Nowitzki layup over Chris Bosh to tie the series at 1-1. Dumping the next game to the Heat, in Game 4 Nowizki again scored the winning basket to even that series at 2-2, even though he was carting around a 101 degree fever. Dallas went on to win the next two games with Nowitzki scoring 62 points in six four-quarters in the 4-2 Championship win over the Heat. Is there any doubt that the Gentle German was named MVP?

The next two seasons belonged to the Heat, and LeBron James is arguably one of the best players of all time. And he's not done yet! In the 2012 NBA Finals, Miami beat the Thunder 4 games to 1. James was named MVP of the series, capping off a season where he hit 19,000 career points. Imagine how many he'll have when he retires! Miami returned the following season, beating the Spurs 4 games to 3 in the 2013 Finals. Again James was named MVP. The Heat almost made it three in a row in the 2014 Finals, but San Antonio got its revenge, beating Miami 4 games to 1. After losing the 2014 Championship, in a highly debated move, LeBron went back to Cleveland. Now we'll see what King James will do with the Cavaliers.

Can't leave out the Celts and Lakers, two teams that have had mega dynasties in NBA history and lots of key playoff moments that had fans on the edge of their seats. How about the Spurs sweeping Cleveland in 2007 for their 4th NBA title in a nine-year span?

Sometimes there are individual performances that standout even if the team goes on to lose that series. For instance, in L.A.'s battle against the Celtics in the 1970s Finals, Laker Jerry West nailed a spectacular 63-foot jumper that tied Game 3. West earned the name "Mr. Clutch" for the shot that people would talk about for years to come. Despite West's effort on the floor, Boston ended up winning that series in a deciding Game 7.

To be sure, there are at least 100 other playoff moments I could have pointed out. These are just a few that make my highlights reel.

9

Show Me the Hall

When everything is left on the hardwoods and it is time to call it quits, NBA superstars are hoping to be inducted into the Naismith Memorial Basketball Hall of Fame in Springfield, Massachusetts. The Hall's location is significant; the building is named after James Naismith. He's credited with inventing the sport at Springfield College back in 1891.

If you make the trip to Springfield, you'll find that the Hall has over 300 people enshrined for their contributions to the sport of basketball. While the players are held to five years after retirement, others admitted into the Hall for what's loosely been termed "contributions to the game," like an owner for example, can be admitted without a set number of years. Herein lies the voting procedures controversy. The Hall of Fame has often been slammed for enshrining active college coaches and some relatively unknown players while leaving other players and even coaches with a long list of accomplishments out.

The very first player inducted into the Hall of Fame was George Mikan in 1959, the first year the Hall inducted anyone. Mikan won championships in several leagues: National Basketball League, the Basketball Association of America, and the NBA. Mikan was one of the original big men of the game at 6'10", 245 pounds. He used his physical attributes for shot blocking and rebounding over the smaller players. His career in the NBL started in 1947 on a team from Chicago, and he quickly went to the Minnesota Lakers. He thrived with the team that became part of the National Basketball Association in 1949, when the BAA and NBL morphed into today's NBA. Minnesota won the first Championship, beating the Syracuse Nationals in six games. Mikan averaged 31 points in the playoffs.

Mikan and 160 other players have been enshrined into the Basketball Hall of Fame. While the vast majorities are from the NBA, certainly not all are, as the Hall includes female players and players from the old ABA or American Basketball Association days. Since the Hall accepts professional and amateurs both in the U.S. and internationally, the selection process is a lot different from, let's say, the Pro Football Hall of Fame. There are people on six different committee's making the selections, and because it's anonymous, there is no arguing on who is chosen and who is left out.

I doubt many people would argue with the selection of Wilt Chamberlin, Bob Lanier, Kareem Abdul-Jabbar, or Magic Johnson to name a few of the usual suspects when it comes to basketball greatness! The referees and amateurs mixed in that you never heard of, I'd say should be left out.

All the classes of Hall of Famers are interesting for different reasons. Take 2011, for instance. Inductees included Denis Rodman, Chris Mullin, and Tex Winters. Rodman, often controversial, was a key contributor on two championship Detroit teams and three Bulls teams that won the NBA Finals. He excelled defensively, especially when it came to rebounds. He seemed to know all the angles the ball would hit coming off of the backboard.

Mullin started racking up the accolades when he was in college. He was named the Big East Player of the Year three times. His all-time scoring record still stands at St. Johns. In 16 years with two teams, Golden State and Indiana, he was an offensive machine. He finished his career with 17,000 points, 3,000 rebounds, and 3,000 assists.

If you've heard of the triangle-post offense you know the name Tex Winter. He received the award posthumously. Winter was part of nine NBA championship teams with both the Bulls and Lakers, and he helped build offenses that stood the test of time. Winter also coached Kansas State, making it into two Final Fours. He started his college coaching career back in 1947.

So, while I don't agree with the wide net the committees cast for the Naismith Memorial Basketball Hall of Fame, I do think it is worth making the trip for any NBA fan. In 2002 the Hall moved into a brand new $48 million dollar state-of-the-art facility that includes a court that visitors can use and a ton of interactive exhibits. Plus the memorabilia is worth the price of admission! Maybe in the future the selection process will become more transparent and the Hall more selective in who makes it into Naismith's Den of Champions.

Invade the Man Cave Tip

If you like loud music and you like to dance, the NBA is for you. The action is fast paced; usually there is a lot of scoring and plenty of musical interludes along the way. The game is pretty easy to follow and if you buy a program, all the rules will be inside of the magazine along with a roster of the players.

PART FOUR

National Hockey League

10

Beyond the Blades

Some blades, a stick, a puck, and a net basically make up the great game of hockey. Spend some time in Canada, and I dare you to find a frozen pond without at least a handful of kids or adults trying to score on the dummy in the nets. I lovingly say "dummy" because I'll never understand how anyone wants to stand crouched in front of a net on ice taking pucks to the face. Never mind that the speed at the professional level sometimes exceeds 100 miles an hour.

One year at the National Hockey League's All-Star Game skills competition, Zdeno Chara, the captain of the Boston Bruins team that won the Stanley Cup in 2011, drilled one puck 105.9 mph. Al McInnis, former defenseman for the Calgary Flames and the St. Louis Blues, generally is regarded as having the all-time hardest shot ever in the game. McInnis, who retired in 2004, would consistently hit his slap shot 95 miles an hour. One time when he was playing with the Flames he hit a shot that nailed Blues goaltender, Mike Liut, on the mask. It split the mask and the puck fell into the net for a goal. Unbelievable!

Hockey is such a fast-paced, physical sport that, without a doubt, speed on the ice is an extremely important weapon. I'd say the New York Rangers Marian Gaborik is the most explosive. He looks like the flash going down the ice. He can make it from end to end in mere seconds. If clocked I bet he's skating 35–40 miles an hour. At laps recorded in training camp a few years ago Gaborik recorded a time of 12.998 seconds.

Over the years, combining some of the skills already mentioned, and adding a few more, there have been players who seem to transcend the sport. Here are a few of mine, and the list includes a few old school guys. Part of my criteria included what they did to advance the game of hockey just by being on the ice.

To me, Maurice "Rocket" Richard was deadly coming down the ice. Goalies who faced Richard described his stare as though he was looking right through them. Richard, who died in 2000, spent his entire career with the Montreal Canadians from 1942 to 1960. He was the first hockey player to score 50 goals in 50 games. The Rocket was a big reason why Montreal won the Cup eight times. He netted 544 goals, an amazing 82 of them in the playoffs.

Canadian Gordie Howe, also known as "Mr. Hockey," flat out makes everyone's list. Howe played for the Detroit Red Wings and Hartford Whalers in the National Hockey League, and also played for the Houston Aeros and the New England Whalers in the World Hockey league. He is the only player to compete in five different decades. He started playing for Detroit in 1946 when he was eighteen years old. Howe set all kinds of records, including being part of a team that finished first in the regular season play for seven straight years. And he won four Stanley Cups all with Detroit. What was truly unique about Howe is the fact that he was ambidextrous. He did a lot of damage from both the right side and the left, perfect for the straight sticks they used to use. Too many records to list but here are a few of Howe's greatest hits: he played in 2,421 games, scored 1,071 goals, and had 1,518 assists. I'm exhausted just thinking about all that ice time.

Bobby Orr played most of his hockey with the Boston Bruins. He joined the league in 1966 and finished his last two seasons, 1977 and '78, with the Blackhawks. Many think he is hands down the greatest hockey player of all time. He was a defenseman who had speed and could score. To this day he is the only defenseman to win the scoring title in the NHL, capturing the Art Ross trophy twice. There is so much that could be said about Orr's contributions to the game of hockey, but his two-way play was what really set him apart. To be a defender who can skate often faster than the competing team's forwards made Orr tough to defend. He won the Stanley Cup twice in his career, both in 1970 and '72. He was named as the most valuable player for both of those Cup series.

Finally, we come to Wayne Gretzky, a man who has a name that absolutely transcends hockey. Nicknamed "The Great One," he lived up to his billing! Gretzky's professional career spanned from 1978 to 1999. You'd need ten trucks to haul all the hardware he collected in his career. He is the only player ever to collect 200 points in a season and he did it four times. How did he do it? Gretzky set himself apart by the way he was able to anticipate where the puck was on the ice. He also was like a stalker behind the net, just waiting to make the right move. Somehow he almost always found the puck and then the net. He set all kinds of scoring records with NHL's Edmonton Oilers and took the team to four Stanley Cup Finals, winning them all. Gretzky was traded to the Los Angeles Kings in 1988. He got them to a final but didn't win. He sure made hockey popular in California!

After the Kings, he went to St. Louis before

finishing his career with the New York Rangers. Wayne Gretzky held forty regular season records and fifteen playoff records. When he retired, every NHL team retired his number 99 jersey. No player will ever have that number again. He was also immediately named to the Hockey Hall of Fame, bypassing the normal three-year waiting period.

Invade the Man Cave Attire

It may seem obvious but make sure you bring a coat, sweater or something warm to wear during the hockey game. I don't care where you live. The ice will melt if the arena's not cold. Sometimes it's hard to see the puck, so always watch the replay on the big screen.

11

Stanley Cup

The Holy Grail and Lord Stanley's Mug are just a few nicknames given to the most coveted trophy in hockey. The cup is named after a former Governor General of Canada, Lord Fredrick Stanley. Hockey has always been part of the culture of the country, and Lord Stanley wanted to see that grow and flourish, even more so back in the late 1800s, in a competition between the top amateur ice hockey teams. Officially the first cup was awarded to Montreal's hockey club back in 1893. Ironically, Stanley didn't get to see the championship game; he was called back to England to succeed his brother as the Earl of Derby.

It all changed by 1914 as there were now professional teams and two different leagues: the National Hockey Association, known today as the NHL, and the Pacific Coast Hockey Association.

These became the two leagues that would battle it out instead of the amateurs. Also hockey teams were starting to form in the United States, and despite some original resistance they were now included in the Stanley Cup playoffs. The first American team to win the Cup was the Seattle Metropolitans.

Here's an interesting fact about the Cup: in its entire history the playoffs have only been canceled twice. Sadly, it happened during its infancy. Two years after the Seattle win they were back to face the Montreal Canadians. The series was a real barn burner but tied at 2-2-1. The final game couldn't be played because of a Spanish influenza epidemic. Several players caught it, and Joe Hall, one of the Montreal players, died. Needless to say, the series was cancelled. The only other time the Stanley Cup wasn't hoisted somewhere on the ice above the players heads symbolizing victory was 2005, the year of the National Hockey League's lockout.

Over the years there were several leagues that competed for the Cup. The deals were so-so crazy. As one league would fold, another would start up, and new leagues were put together. Finally, in 1926, the National Hockey League became the only one competing for the cup with a playoff system that included divisions, teams, and a road map to the Cup.

Not surprisingly, the Montreal Canadians owned the path to Lord Stanley on the ice over the years. The team has won an astonishing 24 times. Another Canadian team checks in second for cups; Toronto has won it 13 times. The U.S. franchise with the most wins is the Detroit Red Wings, last winning it in 2008. The Wings home, Joe Louis Arena, has 11 Stanley Cup Banners hanging from the rafters. Records are one thing, but talking about all-time greatest teams and finals are another. And trust me, no one agrees.

You see, hockey fans are passionate, and I should know, as many nights I could hear my mother yelling at the tube out of frustration while watching the Philadelphia Flyers. I grew up in South Jersey and everyone rooted for the Flyers, even if you didn't know anything about the sport. My second cousin, Carol, married the goaltender for Philadelphia at the time, Bernie Parent. We were young kids, so he was Uncle Bernie to all of us. I tell you this story only because my uncle arguably is one of the greatest goaltenders of all time. He was the net minder when the Flyers won back to back Stanley Cups in 1974 and 1975. Both times he was awarded the Conn Smythe Trophy as the Playoff MVP. In the first series he shutout the Bruins in Game 6, giving Philly its first ever Cup and the series with a 4 games to 2 win. Years later when I was hosting a radio sports talk show, Uncle Bernie and I talked about the series and his career. He told me hands down Bruin Bobby Orr was the toughest guy he every faced.

The following year, the Flyers took on Buffalo in the Stanley Cup finals. The Flyers won the first two games at home and then headed for New York for the next game, which would have a unique place in hockey history. Due to an unusual heat wave, in an arena without air conditioning, the ice rink became filled with fog—so thick you could barely see. Imagine trying to pass a puck down ice or trying to stop one in those conditions. I remember both teams out there with towels trying to dissipate the fog in order to play. The Flyers lost that game and the next one but won Game 5 at home. Heading back to Buffalo, Philadelphia knocked off the Sabers 1-0. The Flyers won the Cup, and Parent, with another shutout, was MVP again.

Those series make history for lots of reasons, including the fact that the Flyers were an expansion team. Also, the team had a reputation as the bad boys in hockey for fighting on the ice; so much so the Flyers were called the Broad Street Bullies. HBO Sports has a great documentary on BSB boys highlighting some of the great personalities of the team.

In my mind there is still nothing like seeing a Game 7 in any sport that has the potential for the showdown game. In the history of the National Hockey League there have been sixteen Game 7's. How about a Seventh game that goes into overtime? The Detroit Red Wings beat the Rangers 4-3 in two overtimes for the 1950 cup, and the Red Wings did it again in 1954 to beat Montreal 2-1 in OT. In 1994, Mark Messier scored the winning goal in the Rangers 3-2 win over Vancouver. In 2011, the Bruins, returning to their first Stanley Cup playoffs since losing to the Flyers in 1972, beat the Canucks 4-0 in Game Seven. Oh what a series! Boston rebounded after losing the first game 1-0 and losing the second game 3-2 in overtime.

Bruin players took the Stanley Cup to clubs, on vacation, and even to lunch. Imagine chowing down on a corned beef on rye and in walks Stanley Cup Series MVP Tim Thomas. Shocked? Don't be, as it is one of the many traditions Cup winning teams enjoy. They get to keep the cup for 100 days, passing it around to every player so they can show it off. There are so many wacky stories about where the Stanley Cup has been in the past. One year Martin Brodeur, the goaltender for the New Jersey Devils, ate popcorn out of it at the movies. Mostly the players drink champagne from the top of the bowl. It's safe to say that the 36-pound trophy has travelled more than any other championship award. You never know where it's going to turn up.

PART FIVE

Horse Racing

12

Kentucky Derby

It's been called the most exciting two minutes in sports and involves the best bunch of three-year-old thoroughbreds in Horse Racing. Every year, the first Saturday in May all eyes are turned to Louisville's Churchill Downs, best known as the home of the Kentucky Derby, to watch one of the oldest horse races in the country.

The track was created in the late 1800s by Colonel M. Lewis Clark, though not officially incorporated as Churchill Downs until 1937. Colonel Clark by the way is the grandson of William Clark. Remember the Lewis and Clark expedition? He made a jaunt of his own to England and France for the two biggest races at the time. First he took in the Epsom Derby, the richest and oldest race in Great Britain. It is worth noting that the first day of this classic race is called "Ladies Day," and the women all pull out their fanciest hats and dress for the occasion.

After being bowled over by the most iconic event in England in terms of sports and the social season, William Clark thought he'd seen the best horse racing event of its time, until he moved on to England's French-speaking neighbors. The Grand Prix in Paris knocked him off his feet, with stands filled with spectators screaming as the horses headed for the finish line. As with the Epsom, the Grand Prix was the premiere event for the horse racing world, especially since the race featured the best thoroughbreds in France and allowed foreign horses to enter the race.

Clark couldn't leave Europe soon enough to bring his idea of melding the two into his own version of the best thoroughbred race in the United States. The second he got back to the States he bugged his cousins John and Henry Churchill for the land they had in Kentucky to build a track. Clark says he couldn't have pulled it off without the help of his family, which is why he paid homage to them by naming the track in Louisville after them. The rest as they say is history. If he had to beg, borrow, and steal, Clark was going to start a tradition in his home state to rival what he had seen in England and France.

The first Kentucky Derby in 1875 featured 15 horses with a crowd of 10,000 people watching "Aristides" gallop across the finish line at a distance of a mile and a half. The Derby, also dubbed the "Run for the Roses," truly has captivated both horse-racing fans and those who watch occasionally. The distance and size of the crowds have changed over the years. Today, the Kentucky Derby is Louisville's biggest event. It is a 1.25 mile race for three-year-old thoroughbreds that is held on the first Saturday in May at Churchill Downs. The Kentucky Derby draws an average of 150,000 visitors each year, including residents, out-of-towners, celebrities, presidents, and even members of royal families.

You can't talk about the Kentucky Derby without mentioning some of the famous thoroughbreds who raced across the finish line and into horse-racing history. "Secretariat" may be the greatest horse to ever win the Kentucky Derby. He certainly was the fastest, sailing down the home stretch and finishing the race in 1:59.40, claiming the title in 1973. The large chestnut colt, nicknamed "Big Red," attracted a lot of attention after his race in Louisville, gracing the covers of *Time* and *Newsweek*. He was the water cooler buzz in the spring of '73 and not just in the sporting world. Secretariat went on to win Thoroughbred Racing's Triple Crown in the United States, meaning the next two biggest races—the Preakness and the Belmont. In a rare feat, he bested his time in every race.

Another horse that captured the nation's attention came seemingly out of nowhere as far as the horse-racing world was concerned. In 2004, leading up to the Kentucky Derby, "Smarty Jones" quietly won all six races he was entered into, including the Arkansas Derby. The horse wasn't the favorite at the Derby but won by 2¾ lengths, landing him on the cover of *Sports Illustrated* and quickly becoming a fan favorite. Smarty Jones set several records that day, including becoming the first undefeated horse to win the Derby since "Seattle Slew" in 1977. And it was the first time in 25 years that a trainer, John Servis, and his jockey, Stewart Elliot, combined for a win in their Derby debut. John is my second cousin and everyone in the family was beyond excited for the win. My grandfather had a "Smarty Jones" hat that he wore everywhere in Tampa—he might have tilted the odds in the next race. Ha! John's underdog horse went on to win the Preakness, the second leg of the Triple Crown, then narrowly lost at the Belmont, just missing a bigger place in history. Thanks to the win in the Derby and all of the attention, Smarty Jones easily became one of the all-time fan favorites. Evidenced by the 120,139 spectators who came to watch the horse race in New York, even today one of the biggest crowds ever to witness a sporting event in that state.

"Barbaro" won the race in 2006, and everyone was talking about the Triple Crown again after watching him win his sixth straight race. He became the sixth undefeated horse to win the Kentucky Derby by pulling away in the last turn and straight away winning the race by 6½ lengths. Sadly, Barbaro's shot at the crown was short lived after a tragic accident at the start of the Preakness, when he broke his leg coming out of the starting gate. The horse died a year later but still lives on in horse-racing lore for his magnificent Derby finish.

There are many more great horses that have run the race, and certainly there will be many more in the future. It's worth noting that Churchill Downs is open for a spring and a fall meet each year. However, the Kentucky Derby Museum next to Churchill Downs is open year-round. The museum houses pieces that reflect the history of the Kentucky Derby as well as the history of thoroughbred racing. One of the best things you can catch while visiting Churchill is the documentary about the Kentucky Derby called, *The Greatest Race,* in its 360-degree theater.

13

Preakness

The third Saturday in May, Pimlico Race Course in Baltimore overflows with horse-racing enthusiasts of all kinds for the running of the annual Preakness Stakes. The attendance for the Preakness only trails the Kentucky Derby. Contending horses cover 9.5 furlongs or 1 mile and 3/16ths in "The Run for the Black-eyed Susans." As with all the Triple Crown races, the distances have changed over the years, and the Preakness is no exception, changing six times until settling in at the current distance set in 1925.

The Preakness can trace its beginnings back to 1873 with just seven starters—the winning horse was a three-year-old named "Survivor" and his owner, John Chamberlain, pocketed just $2,050. Survivor won by 10 lengths, and that margin of victory held up until Smarty Jones won by 11 ½ lengths in 2004. The number of horses sprinting for the finish line has certainly fluctuated every season. Would you believe 26 horses entered the race in 1918 and it had to be run in two divisions? Imagine doing the handicapping on that Preakness! Currently, the Preakness is capped at 14 horses, but usually the number of thoroughbreds ends up being much smaller.

One of the most exciting Preakness races was run in 1978 in a battle between "Affirmed" and "Alydar." The two horses had been rivals since they were two-year-olds, and now on the big stage a year later, the contest between the two thoroughbreds didn't disappoint. After Affirmed won the Kentucky Derby by just 1 and ½ lengths, the anticipation for the meet in Baltimore was at a frenzied pitch. Affirmed beat out Alydar by just a neck, and the crowd went crazy.

It hasn't only been the boys that get them going at the Preakness. Did you know that five fillies have won the Preakness in its 136-year history? The last to do it was "Rachel Alexandra" in 2009, and she was the only horse to ever win it from the farthest outside position. She was named "Horse of Year" that same year after breaking all kinds of records at different tracks across the country.

Some of the significant traditions include the singing of "Maryland, My Maryland," which happens to be the official state song, as the horses make their way to the starting gate. My favorite tradition, and unique to the Preakness, is that as soon as there is an official winner, the horse becomes part of the infield. A painter climbs a ladder and paints the colors of the winning owner's silks, of the jockey and the horse, which becomes part of the famous weathervane until the next Preakness is run. In the Winner's Circle the horse also gets a blanket of yellow flowers with dabs of black lacquer to create the illusion of Black-eyed Susans.

14

Belmont Stakes

The Kentucky Derby might lead things off but it's the Belmont that can change lives. The "Run for the Carnations," or the third jewel of the Triple Crown, takes place each June in New York. It is the oldest race of the three, and over the years the closing race has seen some changes—the biggest being the distance. If you were lucky enough to have a seat in the stands in 1867, the distance you would have watched the horses cover around the track would be a mile and five furlongs. Before 1921, the horses ran clockwise like in England. That's certainly not the case today on the first Saturday in June. Today the horses have to cover a mile and a half. Naturally, like all other races in the United States, the thoroughbreds will move in a counter-clockwise direction. This is a true test of the three-year-olds since a horse has to have the stamina to cover a lot of ground and hit its stride on that final turn to head for the Winner's Circle. Only 11 horses have won horse racing's most prestigious prize—the Triple Crown. Imagine winning all three races, at three different tracks, three different distances in a five-week span!

The first Triple Crown winner was "Sir Barton" in 1919, a horse that covered the mile and 3/8ths race, winning easily. Sir Barton would go on to meet "Man O' War" as a four-year-old in a race in Canada and get severely beaten by seven lengths. That sent Sir Barton out to stud. Today, you can visit the memorial for Sir Barton in Washington Park in the small town of Douglas, Wyoming.

The last horse to win the Triple Crown was "Affirmed" in 1978. Would you be surprised to learn that he was the great-great-great grandson of Man O' War? The take on Affirmed is that not only did this horse have speed, but it had guts too. As a two-year-old, Affirmed captured seven of nine starts under the mount of jockey Steve Cauthen, who was just a teenager. It wasn't a surprise to horse-racing fans that as a three-year-old this horse was in the money in all three races.

Seven horses in the past 13 years have arrived at the Belmont Stakes with wins in both the Derby and Preakness, only to fall short at the deadly distance of a mile and a half. If you're curious about the all-time speed record, that belongs to Secretariat who won the Belmont by thirty-one lengths, finishing the race in 2:24 and leaving all others in the dust.

A big difference in the Belmont from the other two major races is that traditions have fizzled over time. Through 1996, the post parade song was "Sidewalks of New York." The following year and up to 2009, you would hear the theme from "New York, New York." And in 2010 the song changed again to "Empire State of Mind." One thing that remains constant is after the race a blanket of white carnations is draped over the winning horse.

Invade the Man Cave Betting Tip

Don't know much about the horses or pari-mutuel betting? Keep it simple. Win, place or show, which means the horse comes in first, second or third. You don't want to bet the ranch, but look for a long shot for fun, and get everyone with you to pitch in a few bucks on a horse. Kind of like the lottery.

PART SIX

Golf: PGA/LPGA and the Old Guys

15

U.S. Open

Tough pin placements, tough course conditions, and sometimes some of the most spectacular play you'll ever see in professional golf. The U.S. Open is the second major of the year, usually played in the third week of June, and it is open not only to guys who make up the Professional Golf Association (PGA), but any professional or amateur with a handicap of 1.4 or lower who qualifies. Half of the field is already determined by players who are exempt from qualifying for a myriad of reasons, mostly because of a previous win. For example the winners of the U.S. Open for the last ten years or any of the other three majors for the last five years go right to the clubhouse and the practice rounds. What a nightmare compiling all this information must be for the United States Golf Association every year. You need a scorecard before the first round is even under way.

So how did this all start? Officially the Open kicked off in 1895 at the nine hole Newport Country Club in Rhode Island. That's right, nine holes that had to be played four times. It was a single-day, 36-hole tournament. The winner, a twenty-one-year-old Englishman, Horace Rawlins, collected $150 bucks and a gold medal. Rawlins wasn't a surprise since the event was mostly dominated by the Brits in the beginning. However, since 1911 the title for the most part has been won by Americans.

Lately the Irish lads have been making a run at it with Northern Ireland's Graeme McDowell becoming the first European player to win since 1970 when he snatched the prize in 2010 by winning at Pebble Beach in California. His friend and practice partner, also from Ireland, Rory "Big Mac" McIlroy, won the 2011 Open at the Congressional in Bethesda, Maryland. He finished 16-under-par with an eight-shot victory and, at twenty-two years old, he is the youngest winner since Bobby Jones in 1923.

Jones, an amateur from Georgia, is responsible for a huge surge in the popularity of the U.S. Open. He won it four times, the last in 1930, and man was that a hard ticket to get. His victory was probably the sweetest as he made a birdie putt 40 feet from the hole on the 18th at Interlachen Country Club in Minneapolis. He won by two strokes! So many people wanted to get a glimpse of Jones that they bought up all the tickets.

If you don't watch golf already, here are a few big moments that'll make you want to start watching the gentleman's sport that has spanned many eras.

I wasn't around for the Arnold Palmer rivalry with Jack Nicklaus but boy did I hear about them from my grandfather. An avid golfer he was always watching on the final day. In 1962, just two years after Palmer beat Nicklaus for the Open crown, the tides would turn in favor of Nicklaus. Arnie had an army of 10,000 spectators while playing in Pennsylvania, his home state, at the Oakmont Country Club. Nicklaus won in an 18-hole playoff, silencing the crowd and Arnie. This was the first of four Open wins for the "Golden Bear."

Instead of silencing the crowd, Hale Irwin ignited them at the 1990 Open at Medinah Country Club in Illinois. Irwin was trailing by four strokes heading into the last round, but the two-time Open winner who had a penchant for drama knew how to win. He hit a 45-foot birdie putt on the 18th that sent the crowd into a wild frenzy. Irwin ran around the green high-fiving fans. Who says golf is stuffy?

Can you believe I haven't even mentioned Tiger Woods yet? We could talk about his 15-stroke win at the Open at Pebble Beach in 2000, or his win at Bethpage State Park on the Black course with all kinds of wicked elements to deal with—mainly rain and rough—in 2002. Since I was working at WFAN radio in New York City at the time, I was fortunate enough to get to play the course before the guys for a media tournament. Let's just say I practically pulled my shoulder out of its socket trying to drive to some of the greens. Longtime New York broadcaster Richard Neer can vouch for me that the fescue grass was tough. In 2008 at Torrey Pines, Woods wowed the crowd in a sudden-death playoff on the seventh hole with a par over Rocco Mediate's bogey. This, however, was after playing in an eighteen-hole playoff which they finished with even par 71's. The U.S. Open is the only one of the four major championships that goes into the following day if two or more players end up tied after four rounds of play. It's exhausting just thinking about it!

16

Masters

Hands down, the Masters is the hardest ticket in sports to get even if you know someone. It's the first Major of the year in golf, and it is played every year at the Augusta National Golf Club during the first full week in April. This tournament is loaded with more traditions than a cotillion party in the South!

Here's the skinny on the start of this uber-prestigious golf tournament that began back in the '30s. The great Bobby Jones wanted some place to play when he retired and thought a piece of land he found in Augusta was just perfect for a course. He couldn't understand why one hadn't already been built! He hired golf course architect Alister MacKenzie, known for designing several British golf courses, to work his magic. MacKenzie started in 1931, and the first Masters, known then as the Augusta National Invitational, was underway in 1934. Horton Smith won.

When anyone talks about the early years, 1935 is brought into the conversation because of Gene Sarazen's shot heard 'round the world from the Par 5, 15th hole. Standing in the fairway Sarazen pulled out his 4 wood, got every piece of it for a double eagle (2), and went on to force a 36-hole playoff with Craig Wood the next day. Sarazen won the tournament, shocking everyone. So much so, as the legend goes, that Wood had already been handed his check for $1,500 for the win. Oops! Sarazen won 7 Majors in his career and gets credit for inventing a club—the sand wedge.

One of the biggest traditions of The Masters is the presentation of the Green Jacket. Whoever wins the tournament is given the sports coat by last year's winner in a ceremony in Butler Cabin. It's then repeated for the spectators on the 18th tee. This dates back to 1949, and what's interesting is that the player only keeps it for a year then has to bring it back with him to Augusta, Georgia the following year. Speaking of Champions, they have a dinner for just the winners and some members of the Augusta National Golf Course Board, the Tuesday night of the week that the tourney gets underway. I'd love to be a fly on the wall to listen to those conversations!

Here's one of my favorite traditions: the Par 3 tournament is played on the grounds the day before the tournament begins. It's supposed to be social but still gets pretty competitive. It was started back in 1960. The Par 3 course is 1,060 yards, a nine-hole design, built on the grounds in the late '50s. Something else that must be a little nerve racking for the amateurs anyway is the tradition of pairing the U.S. amateur champ with the defending champion of the Masters for the first two days. This was started in honor of Bobby Jones because of his amateur status throughout his career. Trust me, there are countless other traditions too numerous to mention!

Let's talk about the course. Trees, trees, and more trees on the 7,435 yards of play make it more than challenging for the players. Starting with the second shot on the 11th, all of the 12th hole, and the tee shot for the 13th are collectively called "Amen Corner." That should tell you something. Every single hole is named for a tree like "the Golden Bell" which is the aforementioned 12th hole, some say the toughest Par 3 anywhere. It's 155 yards to the green, a very narrow target with water in the front and trouble in the back. Just ask Tom Weiskopf who scored a whopping 13 in 1980. My favorite hole might be number 9, "Carolina Cherry," a 460-yard Par 4 with a green that tilts from the back and is deadly. Hit it wrong and it could roll 50 feet.

You can't talk about the Masters and not mention both triumph and tragedy. Starting with the heartache first, Augusta National has been rough for Greg Norman. The likable Australian nicknamed "the Great White Shark" has been bitten by the

Masters. Larry Mize hit a miracle 45-foot chip right into the cup on the 12th, the second playoff hole in a duel with Norman, who was looking at a birdie putt. Needless to say, Norman was rattled and missed it. Two years later in 1989, he needed a birdie on the final hole to win the Green Jacket, or at least a par to force a playoff. Again Norman choked and Nick Faldo won after a playoff with Scott Hoch.

In 2011, Rory McIlroy, from Northern Ireland, was wowing the crowds with amazing play during his first three rounds. He had a four-stroke lead heading into the final day and finished the day shooting an 80, leaving with no Green Jacket and a look of disbelief on his face. South African Charl Schwartzel finished with four birdies and left with a whole lot of green. American Bubba Watson, a fan favorite, has won it twice, in 2012 and 2014. No wonder, the lefty has one of the longest drives on tour, hitting it an average of 315 yards.

At the 2015 Masters, 21-year-old Jordan Spieth won over the fans by winning the tournament, going wire to wire with the lead. He also tied a tournament record by shooting 18 under for a total of 270, an honor he shares with Tiger Woods, who did it in 1997.

The oldest pro golfer to win was Jack Nicklaus at the age of 46. It was his last win at the Masters, and he's won the most, doing it six times between 1963 and 1986. The youngest to ever win the tournament is Tiger Woods. He was just twenty-one when he won in 1997. Woods has won four times so far, the same amount as Arnold Palmer. Phil Mickelson's earned three Green Jackets, his first in 2004, and oh what a win for the easy-going lefty. He hit an 18-foot birdie putt to beat South African Ernie Els for his first Major championship. Finally, Mickelson wouldn't have to be asked when he was going to win a major anymore. He was dogged for years as being the best player to never win a Major Tournament.

Over the years the course will change, with bunkers and trees being moved and added, making it that much harder for those professionals who are invited to play the Masters. But the time honored traditions will live on.

Invade the Man Cave Day Trip

If you've never played golf, think it's boring and for geezers, you are wrong. You need to experience it first hand by going to a pro tournament. Go to a PGA or an LPGA tourney on a day pass. Drink some iced tea, sit on the grass and watch the pros drive for show and putt for dough, or something like that anyway.

17

Others with Sticks

There are so many legends and stories from the world of golf, and not all of them center around the Professional Golf Association. Would you believe there are at least twenty professional golf tours? Keep in mind a pro tour's main objective is to organize tournament stops, get sponsors and regulate that tour.

While the men have had organized tours since at least the early 1900s, the women had to wait awhile. The Ladies Professional Golf Association (LPGA) was founded in 1950 by a group of thirteen players, including Alice Bauer, Patty Berg, Louise Suggs, Marilyn Smith, and Babe Didrikson Zaharias. The world was especially in love with Babe, whose real name by the way was Mildred. She excelled in golf, track and field, and basketball. This woman was just flat out competitive. She even cut a record for Mercury

Records. Her hit song "I felt a Little Teardrop" was sung in quite a few households.

Babe's popularity grew after she won two gold medals in the hurdles and the javelin and picked up silver in the high jump at the 1932 Olympics for track and field. Her fame really exploded, though, once she took up golf, because she was denied amateur status and had nowhere to compete. She decided to enter the Los Angeles Open, a men's PGA tournament. Babe missed the cut but met her future husband, George Zaharias, at the tourney. Eventually, she got her amateur status back and won 17 straight women's tournaments—a record that will probably stand forever.

After the LPGA was founded, Babe Zaharias became the fastest woman to ever reach 10 wins in just a little over a year. She won the Grand Slam, the three women's majors at the time that included the U.S. Open, the Titleholders Championship and the Women's Western Open. I had the chance to interview Marilyn Smith several times in Dallas, and she told me the other ladies weren't jealous of Babe's success, in fact it was the opposite, as she brought attention to the tour. Smith said one of the funniest things she ever heard Zaharias say was, "It's not just enough to swing at the ball. You've got to loosen your girdle and really let the ball have it." A phrase that has been repeated over and over again, but as Smith said she was quite a character. Combining her amateur and professional wins together she won 82 golf tournaments in her lifetime. Sadly, Babe Zaharias succumbed to colon cancer when she was 45 years old in 1956, but not before leaving an indelible mark on the world of sports and the American culture.

There have been other female golfers who transcended the sport, but other than Zaharias only Swedish golfer Annika Sorenstam has made as big an impact. Like Zaharias did, Sorenstam made history in 2003 when she played in the Colonial, a PGA tour stop in Fort Worth, Texas. She didn't make the cut but won over lots of new fans, especially after PGA pro Vijay Singh was quoted as saying she had no business playing and he hoped she didn't make the cut. Sorenstam retired in 2008 as one of the most successful golfers in history with 72 LPGA wins, including 10 majors and 18 other tournaments. She earned $22 million in prize money, and how 'bout this one? She is the only female golfer to shoot a 59 in competition. Sorenstam is married with two young children and is running several golf-related businesses. What happens to golfers who don't want to retire? The women don't have a senior circuit but the men do.

Here's how it works on the PGA tour. Once the Pros hit 50, they are eligible to compete on the Senior PGA tour. Founded in 1980, it was successful right out of the gate. So many of the well-known names from the previous tour continued on to this next one, including Arnold Palmer. Palmer and others who had already played in a few special events for older golfers, mostly in the 1970s, were still crowd favorites and played some great golf. Now named the Champions Tour, the majority of the tournaments are three rounds instead of the usual four. There are no cuts, and since 2006 players have the choice of riding in a cart.

All of that goes out the window for the five Majors. Here golfers have to play four rounds, must walk and there are cuts. Lots of records have been set on this tour, including Jack Nicklaus making 26 birdies in four rounds in 1990 at the Senior Tournament Players Championship. The guy with the most victories is Hale Irwin with 45; remember we talked about his dramatic finish at the U.S. Open on the regular tour already in this book. Who says these guys can't go the distance? In 2003, Andy Bean drove an average of 344.2 yards throughout the Allianz Championship stop. Speaking of long, both Jim Dent and Jay Sigel in 1996 hit the longest drive ever on tour at 422 yards. Both did it at the Tradition. By the way, neither won the tournament. Instead Jack Nicklaus claimed his 4th win at the fifth major on the Champions Tour. You know the old saying right? You drive for show and putt for dough!

PART SEVEN

College Football

18

Face Painters

This is a name I've given to those rabid college football fans that fill the stadiums across the country week after week, often dressed in team colors from head to toe. Crazy rabid fans that, believe it or not, range in age from 17 to 70; there is no age discrimination when it comes to the hard-core alums.

My first real taste of this was when I was in college at Ohio University in Athens, Ohio. Before you read this and think I'm suggesting that OU fans make my top-ten face painter list, relax, I'm not! I went on a road trip with some friends to the other Ohio school in Columbus, The Ohio State University. They are loud, crazy, and oh so proud at Ohio State Stadium, otherwise referred to as "The Horseshoe."

Let me tell you there is nothing like seeing a game between Ohio State and Michigan, and that's where I found myself, right in the middle of a sea of red. This may be one of the best rivalries in all of college football. Between the Michigan fans singing "Hail to the Victors" at levels I've never heard and the Buckeye fans chanting "Stadium O-H-I-O," I'm lucky I didn't lose my hearing. One of the all-time best games I've ever seen between these teams happened in 2006 when Ohio State beat Michigan 42 to 39.

Lots of the history in college football can be subjective as one would imagine based on your perspective. However, people making a living in college football would tell you that the shootout between the Buckeyes and Wolverines is one of the greatest games ever played. Bo Schembechler, a respected former coach for Michigan for 20 years from 1969 to 1989, passed away the day before the 2006 game at 77 years old. Schembechler had put together an incredible winning record at Michigan during his years there, 194-48-5, but he was also an Assistant Football coach at Ohio State in his early years in college football, working for the legendary Woody Hayes.

No way can I do a face-painter list and leave off Alabama! The iconic cry of "Roll Tide" for the Crimson Tide cannot be denied and these fans are rabid. The history of Alabama, which goes back to 1892, includes 13 National Championships, six of those under the watchful eye of Coach Paul "Bear"

Bryant, who led the charge from 1958 to 1982. To give you an idea of how dominant this team was at times under Bryant, in 1961, the Tide outscored opponents 297 to 25. Alabama not surprisingly that year beat Arkansas in the Sugar Bowl, 10-3 and finished the season at a perfect 11-0, winning the National Title.

Home games for Alabama are wild. Bryant-Denny Stadium in Tuscaloosa seats 101,821 people. It's the fifth largest stadium in the United States. You can always tell if the team has won when you hear people leaving the stadium yelling, "Rammer, Jammer, Yellow Hammer." One of the many familiar chants of the Tide!

Happy Valley, Pennsylvania, the home of the Penn State Nittany Lions, has loads of home field advantage going for it thanks to the faithful fans. The fans have started a trend that has spread in sports by wearing white at home games. It's a White Out with every single fan in the stadium participating. Whether it's the professional or the college games across the board, and not just in football, many fans have adopted this practice especially during playoffs.

Legendary Coach Joe Paterno has coached the Lions for 45 years, winning two National titles in '82 and '86. A new tradition was started by some rabid fans in 2005 when hundreds of them started camping out in tents in front of Beaver Stadium the week before the yearly Ohio State game. It's not unusual to see Joe Paterno or the Blue Band, Penn State's marching band, making their way through "Paternoville," as it has affectionately been dubbed.

Moving from Pennsylvania to Louisiana, I would be shellacked if I didn't mention the LSU fans that flat out create a raucous amount of noise at Tiger Stadium in Baton Rouge with their Tiger Bait chants. Talk to anybody in Louisiana about the 2007 game against Florida to find out just how crazy the fans are for LSU. Before the game against Florida, a hated rival of the Tigers, the students left phone messages for the opposing quarterback, Tim Tebow, and I mean thousands of them. Tebow made an obvious phone hand gesture to the fans at the stadium after one of his touchdowns to gig them back during the game. In the end Tiger fans got the better of the Gators and its quarterback with a 28-24 comeback win.

Also making my face painter list: Florida, Florida State, Notre Dame, Auburn, Michigan, Wisconsin, Oregon, Georgia, and Texas. Don't feel badly if your team didn't make my list. I could write a book on face painters, and the all-time best college football rivalries. There are hundreds of stories and I bet every single college football fan you know has one.

19

Championship Game

College football's first official season is generally considered to be 1869 but only two teams played two games. My home state of New Jersey can boast as being the birthplace of college football. The very first intercollegiate game was played at Rutgers University, the Scarlet Knights taking on the boys from Princeton. Rutgers won 6-4, more like a rugby score which is probably more what the game resembled.

Walter Camp, nicknamed "the Father of American Football," gets the credit for the shift from the rugby scrum to the formations we see today in football. In the late 1800s, he came up with the eleven-man team featuring seven men on the line and four in the back field. He was one of the biggest cheerleaders for the sport, writing about all the excitement in *Harper's Weekly* magazine. He also chose the first All-American team in the sport.

The concept of some sort of a poll to determine a national champion was thought up by Casper Whitney, also a writer for *Harper's* at the time. Along with the polls in Division 1-A football the bowls also started to come along. The first Bowl Game ultimately to determine a national champion was in 1902, when Michigan beat Stanford 49-0. An interesting thing about this lopsided game is that Michigan agreed to put 8 minutes back on the clock to end the Cardinal misery. In fact it was so embarrassing that they didn't hold the Rose Bowl again until 1916! Here's a fun fact about the origin of the word "Bowl" connected to college football. You can credit the Tournament of Roses. Since the stadium in Anaheim was shaped like a bowl it fit the description for the big game.

The game which was becoming incredibly popular was also dangerous for many of the players. So much so that some of the rough hits led to the deaths of some players on the teams. In 1905, President Theodore Roosevelt was tired of reading the obits for young football players, and he threatened to ban the sport. This led to the formation of the National Collegiate Athletic Association, or NCAA, to set up rules for college football and enforce them.

In 1926, Frank Dickinson, an economics professor at the University of Illinois, came up with his own system of determining a national champ based on quality of opponents and scoring differentials. He didn't have a computer so it was all done by hand. He picked championships up to 1940.

By the 1930s, the bowls had really started to take shape. Now besides the Rose Bowl on New Year's Day you had three additional bowls: Cotton, Orange, and Sugar Bowl. Also, some conferences were taking form like the Pacific Coast Conference and the Big Ten. Both agreed to send teams to the Rose Bowl.

Fast forward to 1998 and the formation of the BCS or the Bowl Championship Series, formed by the NCAA to decisively crown a true college football champion. To be eligible for a bowl, a team has to win by at least six games during the season. Then they are invited to a bowl game based on their conference ranking and the tie-ins that the individual conference has to each bowl game. The BCS uses college conferences, computer rankings, newspapers polls, the USA Today coaches' poll, and a series of other things like strength of schedule to determine the bowl teams and the ultimate national champ. The big conferences like the ACC, Big 10, Big 12, Big East, Pac 10, and the SEC automatically are guaranteed at least one spot in the BCS bowls. Over the years there has been plenty of controversy in choosing a national champ, both pre and post BCS system.

In 1991, Miami and Washington both finished the season undefeated and then won their respective bowls. Washington beat Michigan 34-14 in the Rose

Bowl, one of the most lopsided victories in that bowl's history, and the Huskies were declared number one in the final coaches USA Today/CNN Poll. Miami knocked off Nebraska 22-0 to win the Orange Bowl and snagged the Associated Press Poll's number one spot, finishing as National Champs. Both teams finishing a perfect 12-0! Guess who made the trip to the White House? The Miami Hurricanes, but both teams are listed as National Champs that year in almost all historical records of college football.

Finally college football has a playoff system as of the 2014-2015 season. Here's how it works: Four teams play in two semifinal games, setting up the College Football National Championship game. Instead of computer rankings or polls, a 13-member committee selects and seeds the teams. Six bowl games—the Rose, Sugar, Orange, Cotton, Fiesta, and Peach—rotate as hosts for the semifinal games. The venue for the Championship game is bid on by cities, similar to what the Super Bowl does in selecting its host City. In January 2015, Ohio State beat Oregon 42-20 in the first true playoff game with more than 33 million people watching. It was a record for college football on a cable network and a 33% audience increase from the previous year.

Invade the Man Cave Jersey Wearers

Everyone, and I mean *everyone*, I know has either a college football tee-shirt, pajamas, hat or jersey. College football rivalries exist because of deep-seated allegiances to teams, because you went to the school or you adopted the team. It's easy to follow and even more fun to go to a game. Just be careful where you sit.

PART EIGHT

College Hoops

20

March Madness

College basketball might have the magic elixir that other sports crave. A playoff system that gets people who don't even watch during the season excited. It's doesn't hurt that college hoops has a catchy theme that everyone on the planet associates with it alone: "March Madness." If you ever filled out a bracket, you know exactly what I'm talking about.

Don't understand? Let me give you the Cliff Notes version of what happens on the road to crowning a champion. We have to take you back to 1939 when the National Collegiate Athletic Association started its tournament and moved it all over the country so more fans could watch.

It caught on like wildfire by 1975. The teams invited jumped from 25 to 32, gradually increasing to 68 in 2011 with the last four teams playing to make it into the final 64. Finding out what teams get invited to the tournament is a big deal and is now referred to as Selection Sunday. All across the country teams, fans, and anxious family members huddle around the tube, anticipating making it to the Big Dance for a chance to compete in a one-and-done tournament.

However, 32 of those teams gain automatic entry by winning their conference championships. But like the other teams, the conference champs have to wait to find out where they will be seeded and where they will play.

The ten-member basketball selection committee is made up of athletic directors and, yes, conference commissioners throughout Division 1 men's and women's basketball, by the way. Committee members serve five-year terms to give every conference a chance at being part of the process.

It's been estimated that 100 million people fill out brackets, and I have a theory why. I know there is often money attached, whether it's five bucks or more to turn in a bracket to your office mate running the pool. Who doesn't want a little extra lunch money? I think following all the teams leads to some interesting competition among those playing as you go round after round, either picking up points or losing them with the teams you chose.

Listen, when I was on the Ticket radio station in Dallas, Texas, my producer thought it would be fun to enter one of the ESPN contests. We did! I actually won the division. I got a leather jacket and a trophy but, more importantly, bragging rights.

So I could bury you with even more mathematical jumping jacks and minutiae but I'll just cover a few memorable highlights instead. Let's dive into some of the amazing finishes.

Take 2015 with the Kentucky Wildcats, the odds-on favorite to make some serious history. Coach John Calipari's and his team took a perfect season into the NCAA Tournament. They seemed like a team of destiny and so many people jumped the gun thinking the Wildcats were a sure thing to go 40-0 and win the Final Four. In the Elite 8, they got a scare with Notre Dame almost knocking them off but pulled it out 68-66. Then along came the Wisconsin Badgers, a great team with one of the best college players: Frank Kaminsky, winner of the John R. Wooden Award and many others. Kaminsky did what he need to on the floor with 20 points and 11 boards. In a grind-out battle, the Badgers beat the Wildcats 71-64. Kentucky went 38-1, still a great season but not enough to eclipse Indiana's perfect season and championship '75-'76.

In the 2015 NCAA Championship, Wisconsin went on to challenge Duke for the title, and it made for an awesome finish. After the Blue Devils polished off Michigan State, Duke coach, Mike Krzyzewski, was on the brink of making history with his 5th win at the helm. The Badgers didn't make it easy, as the game came down to the wire. Credit should go to Duke's Tyus Jones and Grayson Allen; the two combined for 29 of Duke's 37 points after the half. The deadly backcourt overcame a nine-point, second-half deficit and Duke beat Wisconsin 68-63. Coach K, in 35 years of leading Duke, now has 5 Championships in his 12 appearances.

As with every sport, depending on where you went to school or live, the team you root for is always the favorite to win. The great thing about March Madness is the upsets, the unexpected underdogs beating the truly great teams. I picked a few historical upsets, and you might disagree, but keep in mind it would take 1,000 pages to highlight all the legendary games. These are in no particular order.

I watched the 1993 NCAA Championship game in disbelief, probably like so many others. I actually had the good fortune of having Dickie V on my first Sports Radio show that year at KUHL in Santa Maria, California. There was no Red Bull at the time but I swear he was amped up on some sort of energy drink.

So the '93 Championship comes down to North Carolina and Michigan. The Wolverines rallied big time to trim the deficit against the Tar Heels to 73-71, until a fateful timeout called by Michigan All American Chris Webber. As he was being trapped with 11 seconds to play he motioned to stop the clock. Sadly, Michigan was out of timeouts. In the end North Carolina beat Michigan 77-71.

The 1983 Championship game was a tale of desperation shots hitting the mark. Wolfpack sophomore forward Lorenzo Charles scored two key points, converting teammate Dereck Whittenburg's off-line shot into a dunk. North Carolina beat Houston 54-52. This was a heavily favored Cougar team with Clyde Drexler and Hakeem Olajuwon. I'm sure if you were too young to remember, you've probably seen the footage of Wolfpack Coach Jimmy Valvano running all over the court looking for someone to hug.

The year before in 1982, North Carolina freshman guard Michael Jordan nailed a 16-foot jumper with 16 seconds left in the game to knock off Georgetown 63-62. Mentioning two big Tar Heel victories, I have to pause to talk about the legendary coach of North Carolina, Dean Smith.

Smith, who passed away in 2015, coached some of the all-time greatest NBA players, but probably none bigger than Michael Jordan. When Smith died, Jordan said he was family and credited Coach Smith for teaching him basketball. Smith coached from 1961 to 1997 and finished with 879 wins, won the regular season Atlantic Coast Conference 17 times, won the ACC tourney 13 times, went to the NCAA tournament 27 times, made it to 11 Final Fours, and won those two titles I mentioned in 1982 and 1993.

You couldn't possibly write anything about great NCAA Championship finishes and not include

UCLA and the great Bruin coach, John Wooden. Take 1965, when Bruin's guard Gail Goodrich became the only guard to score more than 35 points in a championship. His stats were unbelievable—42 points total on 12 of 22 field-goal shooting and 18 of 20 free-throws made. UCLA knocked off Michigan 91-80.

Coach John Wooden, nicknamed the "Wizard of Westwood," capped off his career at UCLA with a 92-85 win over Kentucky. Coach Wooden won 10 Championships in 12 years, including an unprecedented seven in a row. What's so crazy is that he never made more than $35,000 dollars a year as a coach. When he retired, UCLA gave him a powder blue Mercedes after coaching the Bruins from 1948 to 1975. Thank goodness the brilliant motivator had camps and speaking engagements to round out his calendar and help fill his wallet.

Another one of my favorite games was the 1985 Championship that came down to two big teams out of the East: Villanova took on Georgetown. The Wildcats were the underdogs coming into the finals as an 8th seed out of the Southeast Regionals. Coach Rollie Massimino told his team they would have to be perfect on this April Fool's Day and they were close. Villanova did it by shooting 78.6 percent from the floor against the top-ranked Hoyas. Some people think this is one of the biggest upsets in the history of the tournament with the unlikely run of Villanova, in the end beating the Hoya's 66-64.

Let's not leave out the women who have had some amazing teams and coaches over the years. At the top of any list would be Pat Summitt, who consistently led the Tennessee Lady Vols to the Promised Land. In fact, she is the all-time winningest coach in NCAA history in any division, by the way, in either the men or women's programs.

Summitt coached at Tennessee from 1975 to 2012 and won 8 NCAA Championships, and her overall coaching record was 1,098 wins and just 208 losses. There were many great players and wins of Pat Summitt's era. I'll pick my favorite.

In 2008, the Lady Vols won four straight games in the NCAA Tournament heading toward a Final Four appearance against LSU. Down to the just 0.7 seconds left in the game, Alexis Hornbuckle tipped in a Nicky Anosike missed layup to win the game 47-46. The Vols then went on to beat Stanford 64-48 for Summitt's 8th and final championship.

In the summer of 2011, Summitt announced that she had early on-set Alzheimer's but still remained as part of the coaching staff in a lesser role for the upcoming season. She was awarded the President Medal of Freedom in 2012 by President Barrack Obama and was beaming from ear to ear. Legendary Indiana coach Bobby Knight summed it up best when asked who he thought was the best college basketball coach of all time besides himself. Of course, he said

Pat Summitt.

Besides Summitt, without a doubt Geno Auriemma, the coach of UCONN Huskies, has earned a reputation as one of the best college hoop coaches period. By beating Notre Dame in 2015, not only did the team win its third straight NCAA Championship, but Auriemma tied John Wooden's record of 10 wins. Auriemma's been the coach at Connecticut since 1985 and will most certainly challenge Pat Summitt's overall record as he continues to groom his Huskies year after year to make it to the championship game. It's only fitting since he had such a huge rivalry with Pat Summitt throughout the years. My favorite Geno win was in 2003 when UConn beat Tennessee 73-68. Oh, the icy stare from Pat Summitt could put anyone in an instant freeze.

As with college football, I have never met more passionate fans than in the sport of college basketball. Perhaps it has to do with going to the school and being a part of your team's culture, or growing up and rooting for the team where your parents went to college. For that reason, many of you reading this chapter might be wondering, why didn't you talk more about Michigan or Notre Dame or ...? Well, you get my drift. It would be impossible to cover all the great teams, players, coaches, and moments in this book. But these were the greats that stood out for me.

PART NINE

Left Turns: Auto Racing

21

NASCAR and IRL

I am proud to say I am a fan of the left-turn sports but this wasn't always the case. I'm guilty of being like those people who say that they don't like hockey even though they have never been to a game. Wheel sports are the same way. Once you go, you feel an excitement in the air that just can't be matched when you're plopped on the couch with your feet up, eating chips and drinking a cold one. By the way, I know some of you will disagree!

Speed, strategy, pit stops, and drivers you hate, plus drivers you love and lots of laps. In a nutshell that was my experience when I had the chance to watch the sport up close, and I have to say I was blown away. By the way, I'm talking about both the National Association for Stock Car Auto Racing (NASCAR) and the Indy Racing League (IRL). Both types of racing center around the basic premise of a driver going fast on a track and after a certain amount of laps taking the checkered flag at the finish line. But there is a world of difference between the two.

NASCAR, hands down, is a fan favorite as television ratings don't lie. It stacks up second to professional football. Maybe I need to take back what I said about couch potatoes watching racing all day. The other big thing is the incredibly loyal fans that spend money on the sport. NASCAR can not only boast of having the best attendance of almost all single-day sporting events in the world, but it's also a sport that rakes in over $3 billion in licensed products sold.

So how did this all start? In Daytona Beach, Florida it wasn't just about the waves, surf, and girls in bikinis. You also wanted to have a fast car. Trying to set land speed records, all kinds of drivers raced on any two-mile stretch of beach or very narrow blacktop that was part of the beachfront highway, connected by turns made of sand at the end. That course was calling out to auto mechanic William France, Sr. who moved from Washington, D.C. in the grips of a Great Depression to Florida. France liked speed and driving so he entered the 1936 Daytona race, which was a little longer than a couple of miles. It was supposed to be 250 miles but lasted only 10 miles. Most of the cars broke down because some drivers were in cars that were just too heavy and got caught up in the sand.

France decided to run the so called beach race, promoting it wherever he could and decided that people would like watching stock car racing with the right venues and some sort of rules. France found the right mix of drivers and promoters, and NASCAR was officially born years later in 1948. There was a standardized set of rules, scheduled stops or races, and a championship! My favorite story is the meeting where the point system was written down on a napkin from the bar. Oh how far the sport has come!

In the beginning there were three different divisions: the modified, roadster, and strictly stock. Roadster flopped and was dropped. However, Charlotte Speedway hosted the first-ever strictly stock race which is still popular today. Driver Jim Roper was declared the winner of the race in 1949 after another driver altered the rear springs in his car. Things really exploded decades later in 1972, as the Cup series was shortened to 31, down from the nearly 48 previously in the series. Really, this was what some people call the modern era of NASCAR. There were certainly a lot of personalities in the sport, guys like Richard "the King" Petty. He won the Championship Series seven times and the Daytona 500 seven times. Retired now at 74 years old, he raced in 1,184 races over 35 years. Can you imagine?

The Petty's have a long history in the sport. Richard's father Lee won the very first Daytona 500 back in 1959, and obviously the apple doesn't fall far from the tree. His son, Kyle, also raced and is now a successful commentator on a few top NASCAR television shows. Sadly, Kyle's son Adam, the first fourth-generation driver in the sport was killed during practice in 2000 at New Hampshire Motor Speedway. He was just 19 years old. He came to my studio when I did a sports radio talk show in Dallas, Texas, and what a delight this kid was, talking about getting ready to race at the Texas Motor Speedway. Adam Petty was trying to qualify for the Winston Cup. He did it finishing 40th overall with engine problems slowing him down.

My favorite driver was Dale Earnhardt. Flat out like Petty, he was a monster competitor, winning seventy-six races, but only one Daytona 500 in 1998. Not surprisingly, the man nicknamed "the Intimidator" won seven championships and tied Richard Petty for the most all time in the sport. Right from the get-go Earnhardt was good. In his rookie season he won a race at Bristol, won four poles, had 17 top-ten finishes and finished 7th in the point standing even though he missed a few races because of injury. A year after Adam Petty died at the beginning of a promising career, Earnhardt was killed in a last lap crash during the 2001 Daytona 500. He was just 49 years old.

Today, the NASCAR Sprint Cup Series is the most popular, with 36 races held over 10 months on tracks across the United States. The series gets better and better with rule changes and a revamped point system that includes points for not just winning a race but coming in second, third and so on plus leading a lap and leading the most laps in a race. This gives all the drivers a chance, even if they don't win a lot of races, and it's also more interesting for the fans.

We shift from NASCAR to IRL and move from stock cars to open-wheel racing. The early years of Open Wheel could be traced back to 1905 to the American Automobile Association, the first sanctioning body for auto racing in the United States. Fast forward a few years to the American Championship car racing. Around since 1916, it basically included any pro racers of single-seat open-wheel race cars. The history is somewhat convoluted with several different sanctioning bodies trading places. In the late '70s, Championship Auto Racing Teams (CART) was founded, sliding into the spot of United States Automobile Club. Most of the drivers who won the races were from America. Pay attention as this will mean something later.

If all of this has you dizzy you're not alone. Let's put it this way, CART filed a lawsuit against the Indianapolis Motor Speedway to try and protect their license to the Indy Car mark in 1996. The upshot is it ultimately led to no CART teams or drivers competing in the Indy 500 from 1997 to 1999. It would take a book on just the myriad of things going on in Open Wheel at the time to explain the breakdown of teams, drivers, the Indy 500 plus the assorted political nonsense. Just for the sake of accuracy, the Indy Racing League was officially founded in 1994 by Tony George and started racing in 1996.

Needless to say CART had all the biggest drivers but slowly the Indy Racing League, which only had three races including the Indy 500 in 1996, started to add races. CART went down the tubes in 2003, declaring bankruptcy. Many say the IRL/CART breakup is why there was an overall lack of interest in open-wheel racing. While the sport has unified its leagues as of 2008, it happened perhaps too late in the game. There are fewer teams, many more foreign drivers, plus a series of races that aren't on ovals but road courses. Americans like their left turns on a track.

22

Wheels

Remember that line from the '80s movie *Top Gun* when Maverick turns to Goose and says, "I feel the need . . . the need for speed."? Truly that's what racing is all about from hot rods and stock cars to open-wheel rides. Qualifying for Indy Cars range from 215 to 227 miles an hour but average about 207 mph for the race. It's a little different in NASCAR; they hit up to 191–195 mph in qualifying, and the average speed will vary from 130–170 mph. However, it depends on the track, and sometimes the racing officials try and step in to slow things down.

Let's talk about a few of the big races and we'll start with NASCAR. I love that the Super Bowl of the sport is at the beginning of the season with the Daytona 500. It is 500 miles and 200 laps of pure wall-to-wall racing out at the Daytona International Speedway. One of my favorite traditions of this race is that the winning car, in whatever shape it's in after the race, is displayed for one year at the Speedway's museum next door to the track. The winner's check, $1,463,810, in 2011 went to Trevor Bayne. Starting 32nd in the race, his average speed in his number 21 Motorcraft/Quick Lane Ford Fusion was 130 mph, and he finished in 3:59:24. He is the youngest driver to win the race at twenty years old.

The record for the fastest time was set, believe it or not, back in 1980 by Buddy Baker. In his number 28 Oldsmobile, he started on the pole and never looked back until he hit the checkered flag. Baker was edged out in 1983 by Cale Yarborough, the first guy to run a qualifying lap over 200 miles an hour. Too bad he flipped his Chevrolet Monte Carlo on the second lap of qualifying and had to race a back-up, a Pontiac LeMans. He made his move when he had to and passed Baker on the last lap to win.

In 1997, Jeff Gordon won the race in his 24 Chevrolet, under a caution flag. He became the youngest driver to claim the top spot. At the time, he was twenty-four years old. So far in his career, Gordon has finished in the Top Ten 382 times, has claimed 70 poles and 84 wins, including three Daytona 500 victories.

Jimmie Johnson won the 2006 Daytona 500 with Hendricks Motorsports just like Gordon in his number 48 Chevrolet, and oh what a good omen! Johnson made history by being the only driver to win the Sprint Cup Championships for five straight years from 2006 to 2010.

Now we take an abrupt turn to the Indianapolis 500 for a different race at the Indianapolis Motor Speedway, also rich with tradition. It was built in 1909 as a gravel-and-tar track, but after two fatal mishaps the asphalt had to go—replaced instead with bricks—3.2 million of them and a concrete wall around the outside of the track. The Indy 500 is known as "the Greatest Spectacle in Racing" and is held each year on the Sunday before Memorial Day. Whoever wins usually leaves with a milk mustache, as the tradition is to drink milk after the win. The Speedway's website boasts to fans that you could fit Churchill Downs, Yankee Stadium, the Rose Bowl, the Roman Coliseum, and Vatican City all inside the oval. They say if the seat boards from the grandstands at IMS were laid end-to-end they would stretch 99.5 miles. Size does matter at Indy and, hands down, they have it!

A.J. Foyt, Al Unser, and Rick Mears are all tied in the history books for the most wins with four, and Penske Racing Team can claim victory for its drivers 15 times. Foyt has one other distinction worth noting besides his Indy wins. He has won the Daytona 500, the 24 Hours of Daytona, and the 24 Hours of Le Mans. No longer driving, like many others in the racing game, he is an owner and has had teams in IRL and NASCAR racing for A.J. Foyt Enterprises.

In all, 70 drivers have won the Indianapolis 500, including Helio Castroneves from Brazil, who has never finished lower than sixth in IRL standings. Castroneves took the flag in 2001, along with Indy 500 Rookie of the Year. He also won in 2002 and 2009. He may have one of the all-time best nicknames in racing—"Spider-Man"—as his tradition when he wins is to climb up the track-side debris fence, and the fans go wild.

No matter what the race or where it's held, drivers know there is someone out there dying to take a crack at qualifying. Only a few will come down that straight away to hear the thunderous roar of some of the most passionate fans in sports, both in Indianapolis and Daytona.

Invade the Man Cave Tip

If you go to a race in person, get a headset so you can hear the driver conversations with the crew. It's legal eavesdropping. Races are loud, fast and it's a long day, so bring plenty of snacks or be prepared to hit the concession stands a bunch.

PART TEN

Tennis: Big Gamers

23

Down Under, on Clay in France, and Hard Courts in the U.S.

The Australian Open is the first major tennis tournament of the year, so why would any tennis professional with a big game not make the trip to Australia? Believe it or not, over the years it was tough to get commitments from anyone, let alone stars, so the draws were weak. Think about this, if you wanted to play in 1920, the trip from Europe by ship to Australia took about 45 days. So months were taken up to earn just a fistful of dollars, and that's if you even won! Even crazier, the tournament committee had a hard time making its mind up about where to play it, holding the Open in seven different cities in the country, five of them in Australia and two in New Zealand.

Today, while most big gamers make the trek to Australia, they certainly complain, although it's mostly about the fact that it falls mid-January every year when they still want more downtime. To ease the whining, the prize money was sweetened! The male or female who wins Down Under will walk away with $2.2 million. I'd say that's some incentive.

The tournament has been played at Melbourne Park for the last twenty years and is one of two Grand Slam venues, with a few show courts that have a retractable roof. The other is Wimbledon, by the way, which makes sense given all the rain in England. In Australia, rain is certainly a huge possibility that time of year but the heat is the real killer. It's not unusual for players to get sick with the hot temps, because they are constantly hydrating. While the players might be sucking up all the water they can find, the courts don't have to be watered. The Aussie's ditched the popular grass surface for the hard courts when they moved to Melbourne.

Now, let's talk records. On the men's side, Australian Roy Emerson racked up the hardware, winning six tournaments in the '60s. After Emerson, American Andre Agassi and Swiss star Roger Federer both claimed first prize four times. Agassi loved the Aussie Open, and the crowd liked his swagger and massive returns. Give Agassi a 150-mile-an-hour serve, and I swear he would find a way to get it back. Okay, slight exaggeration but you get my drift. Federer, who last won in 2010, is a machine in his own right, with a killer forehand that seems effortless. He may go down in history as the greatest player of all time. We'll see what his stats look like when he retires.

On the ladies side, it was Australian Margaret Court winning the most singles titles, with seven to her credit. Court won all four majors in 1970, a Grand Slam accomplishment—all in the same calendar year. American Serena Williams won the tournament five times and has no trouble making the trip to the "Land Down Under." German Steffi Graf has also won the Australian three times and, like Court, Graf can boast about the rare Grand Slam. She did it in 1988.

Now, we move from the land of the Koalas and Kangroos to France and a big-game tournament for clay lovers. A surface that is embraced by some, like current champion and "the King of Clay" Rafael Nadal, who has won the French Open six times; and hated by others, like American Pete Sampras, one of the greatest to play the game. He retired in 2002 having set all kinds of records and winning over $43 million in prize money. But he could never win on the red clay in Paris.

The French Open was open to all amateurs starting in 1925. Before that, only tennis players who were members of French clubs were allowed to compete. If you go to Paris for the tournament at the end of May–early June, you'll hear the French refer to it as "Roland Garros," named for a famous World War I pilot. That's where the tournament is played.

A quick word about the red clay. The play is much slower and very physically demanding. You'll see players often use the surface to slide into shots.

Here are some of the records; since sports are always about the numbers: Frenchman Max Dacugis won the most, but that was back in the amateur days starting with his first win in 1903. Wonder what the crowds were like in those days? Swedish Superstar Bjorn Borg, with his killer two-handed backhand, won six. Nadal, as previously mentioned, just tied Borg's record.

The ladies have records to brag about, as well, on the clay. In the 20s, French woman Suzanne Lenglen was hard to beat, winning six times, while American Chris Evert actually has the most singles titles with seven. She's also the oldest woman to win on clay, claiming her last win at thirty-one years old in 1986. Even more remarkable about Evert, and a little known fact for some reason, is her career winning percentage of .900. She won 1,309 matches and lost only 146 in her career, before retiring in 1989. Steffi Graf also won the tournament six times, almost tying Evert's seven wins, but was knocked off in the finals in an amazing three-set final won by Yugoslavian Monica Seles in 1992. The score: 6-2, 3-6 and 10-8.

Now grab your suitcase as we jump over the pond and back to the United States for the final Grand Slam: the U.S. Open. I reserve the right to jump out of chronological order as Wimbledon, the most prestigious of the all of the slams, gets a few extra pages. Man, I can just see the e-mails pouring in, but read on and you'll understand.

Each year in the beginning of September, New York City comes alive with the big gamers in tennis making their way to Queens and the U.S Open. I get goose bumps just thinking about the trips I've made, having the fortunate pleasure of covering this tournament seven times in my career.

For some fresh off the sting of a loss on the hallowed lawns of Wimbledon, the U.S. Open is about redemption. For others it is about dominance. Fates and fortunes can change on a dime in the city that never sleeps. Let me introduce you to a few tennis players who would probably agree with me.

In the first few years of the tournament in the 1880s, the U.S. Open was only open for men, and only those who belonged to the United States National Lawn Tennis Association. And it was actually held in Newport, Rhode Island. Afterwards, the tournament moved to Forest Hills of Queens, New York then to Philadelphia. We need a scorecard to keep up with these moves!

Since the Open Era in 1968, it has been held in New York, first on the grass of the West Side Tennis Club, and now it is played on hard courts at what is now the USTA Billie Jean King Tennis Center. What is unique to the tournament is the scoring. It's the only Grand Slam still using the tie break in all sets, including the final one. All the other tournaments keep playing until a winner is declared after winning the decisive set by at least two games. For example, remember when I talked about the French final between Seles and Graf? The final set and the tournament were won by Monica Seles with a score of 10 to 8.

Let's talk about champions. For the men one of my favorites, going old school, is Jimmy Connors, who won the Open five times! Here's a fun sports trivia fact for you: Connors is the only tennis player to win the Open on all three surfaces—grass, clay, and hard court. His last U.S. Open victory was in 1983, but the match everyone remembers was the match he played the 1991 semi-finals on his 39th birthday. He beat 24-year-old Aaron Krickstein 3-6, 7-6, 1-6, 6-3, 7-6. It took 4 hours and 41 minutes. Plus Connors was down 2-5 in the final set before winning it. The crowd went wild! He lost in the next round but it didn't matter. It's still a match that is replayed and talked about today. Years later I had the good fortune of having a conversation with Connors about that moment, and he said he felt the vibration from the crowd. Pete Sampras and Roger Federer have won the tourney five times in their careers.

As for the women: Chris Evert won the U.S. Open six times but could have had two more if not for Martina Navratilova, Evert's biggest rival. Martina thrashed her in 1983, 6-1, 6-3 and then went on to beat her again in '84 in maybe one of their most exciting matches 4-6, 6-4, 6-4. You can't talk about the women and not mention Billie Jean King. She won the Open four times. King paved the way for women, and not just in tennis, when she founded the World Tennis Association and pushed for equal prize money for women. She has dedicated her life to tennis, helping both women and men. She was recognized in 2006 by the United States Tennis Association (USTA), when they renamed the grounds of the U.S. Open tennis center after her. Now it's the USTA Billie Jean King National Tennis Center.

So many champions past and present have accomplished amazing things in the Big Apple; way too numerous to mention here. If you ever have the chance, I urge you to go grab a ticket and catch the fever yourself with a trip to the U.S. Open. You can be certain with big prize money, a big city, a big attitude, many great champions will continue to make their way to New York to put the icing on the cake or start a great career.

24

Wimbledon

The biggest gamers in tennis are all hoping for one thing every year when they arrive at the All England Lawn Tennis and Croquet Club—to win the most prestigious professional tennis tournament in the world. Unique to this Grand Slam is its surface—grass. All the majors except the French Open, which has always been played on clay, used to be on grass but switched to hard courts. The first Wimbledon was played in 1877 and was limited to men's singles. Only 22 competed and fans paid one shilling at the time to watch. Spencer Gore won that year. He was an amateur, as all the players were, until the beginning of the Open Era in 1968.

The lawns were arranged so there would be a "Center Court" surrounded by all the other courts. In all, there are nineteen, but what's interesting is that Center Court and Number 1 Court are considered to be the show surfaces and are only used during the Wimbledon Championships. The rest of the time the ryegrass is off limits, except when London hosts the 2012 Olympics.

The tournament takes place at the end of June and beginning of July for 13 days, and is one of the hardest tickets in sports to get. It is chock-full of traditions, including the wearing of white, a must for all the players who compete in the tourney. Chances are, those who have a front row seat will be eating strawberries and cream, the main dish at the Wimbledon.

If those courts could speak . . . oh, what stories they would tell of the blood, sweat, and tears left behind. Some of the greatest matches ever played in the history of tennis have been played on the grass in England. The best of all-time arguably could be the Rafael Nadal-Roger Federer final in 2008. You didn't dare leave your seat no matter where you watched. Nadal won the first two sets 6-4, 6-4, but Federer roared back to win the next two sets 6-7, 6-7, and the final set could have gone either way. Plus rain delays and impending darkness threatened to call the match. In the end Nadal pulled it out 9-7 to win his first Wimbledon, and Federer, racked with emotion, was saddled with the loss. The Spaniard ended Federer's run of five consecutive Wimbledon titles and 65 straight wins on grass courts.

Equally as thrilling was the 1980 match featuring

John McEnroe and Bjorn Borg—another five-setter pitting two rivals with contrasting styles. Borg was the ice man who played with no emotion, and McEnroe was the opposite—the guy who yelled at the lines people and argued calls all day long. Even when he walked on Center Court, McEnroe was booed, mostly as retribution for his nasty exchanges with officials in his semi-final against Jimmy Connors. McEnroe won the first set 6-1, and then Borg roared back to grab the next two sets 7-5, 6-3. In the fourth set Borg had a chance to close it out. McEnroe saved five match points and eventually won 18-16. The fifth set went to the steely-eyed Swede, 8-6.

Here are some other records of big gamers: American Pete Sampras holds the record for the most wins on the men's side with seven, his last in 2000. Bjorn Borg and Swiss star Roger Federer each have five trophies.

Wimbledon has also featured some huge matches and rivalries on the ladies side. Martina Navratilova has won on the grass more than anyone else with nine titles. Her closest rival, Chris Evert, won the tournament three times. Martina had the edge in the overall match count 43-37. In an interview I did with Navratilova, she said, without a doubt, Wimbledon was her favorite place to play and where she truly felt comfortable. Those results don't lie!

The Williams sisters have dominated at the All England Club in recent years: Serena has won it five times, the last time in 2012. Big sister Venus has also won it five times. Serena beat Venus three times in England in the finals with Venus snagging the win from her once in the finals. Imagine playing your sister for eight Grand Slam titles, which includes Wimbledon! Overall in their careers, Serena has the edge, winning six times, beating Venus 13 times out of the 23 matches they've played against each other. There have been many other stars on the grass, and there will be many more in the future vying for the right to be called Wimbledon Champion. Right now every year, 128 men and women fight for the slots on any of the grass courts. Only two will walk away with a million-dollar-plus check and trophy.

PART ELEVEN

Sports of All Sorts

25

Olympics

Dah . . . dah . . . dah . . . dah . . .

I'm no music major but the Olympics are so ingrained in our brain. Can't you hear that familiar opening theme for the broadcast? It actually has a name; it's called "Bugler's Dream." How many kids have hopes of making it to the Olympics?

As far as I'm concerned, the Olympic Games, featuring thousands of athletes from more than 200 countries competing in all sorts of sports, is the biggest international sporting event. It's pure brilliance, if you think about how the games were inspired by the Olympic competitions in Greece, dating back to 8th Century BC through the 4th Century AD. The rebirth started with the formation of the International Olympic Committee in 1894. Currently, the Olympics occur every four years with the summer and winter games alternating every two years.

The Olympics pull us in with athletes who thrill

us with their performances and the overall medal count. The United States usually finishes at the top of the leaderboard, but at the Winter Games in Sochi Russia in 2014, it was the host country that ended up with the most medals at 33 overall to America's 28.

One of the best Gold Medal moments from those games for me was a 20-year-old snowboarder. No one expected Sage Kotsenburg to come out of the gate and smoke the competition the way he did. He nailed the Snowboarding Slopestyle with a laid back solid performance that put him on the podium with a gold medal around his neck, listening to "the Star Spangled Banner."

We could spend days arguing about the all-time best Olympic moments. After all, how do you come up with criteria that make sense and take into account all the eras, plus summer versus winter Olympics? So keep that in mind as I toss out some of the best moments in no particular order.

Swimmer Michael Phelps would have to be at the top of any list, especially after his performance at the Beijing Olympics in 2008. He won 8 gold medals, breaking fellow American Mark Spitz's record of 7 golds set back in 1972. Overall, Phelps has won 22 medals, and 18 of them are gold from 4 career trips to the Olympics. Phelps has retired from swimming after a life of logging miles and miles in the pool, but some say he may surprise us and make it to Brazil in 2016. Can you imagine?

Sticking with the summer games from another era, I have to give it to Michael Johnson. In the Track and Field competitions, he won two gold medals, absolutely crushing two world records. In the 400-meter race, he flew around the track in 43.49 seconds to a wild U.S. crowd in Atlanta. Then with just a few days in between, he sauntered onto the track to take gold in the 200-meter sprint, making history by becoming the first man to win both races in the same Olympics. I had the opportunity to speak with Michael years later, and he told me he knew he had something special left in the tank. He sure did!

Jamaican Usain Bolt has the perfect name. If you watched him in 2008 at the Beijing Olympics, you saw magic on the track. He broke the world and Olympic records in both the 100-meter and 200-meter events. He also set a 4x100 meter relay record on the Jamaican team. He became the first man to win three sprinting events at an Olympics since American Carl Lewis did it in 1984.

You can't talk about the Olympics and not mention some of the amazing gymnastic feats. Romanian gymnast Nadia Comaneci won three gold medals in 1976 at the summer games in Montreal. She also became the first female gymnast to ever be awarded a perfect 10 in the Olympics.

Then along comes 16-year-old American Mary Lou Retton and her mind blowing performance in the 1984 Olympics. She became the first American female (or male) to win a gold medal in gymnastics. She closed the deal with perfect 10s for a stellar performance on the vault.

Speaking of firsts for Americans and the Olympics in gymnastics, almost nothing was better than watching Kerri Strug in 1996. She stuck her second landing off the vault, despite her injured ankle. Strug had to be carried to the podium by her coach Bela Karolyi. Thanks to nailing that landing, the U.S. women beat the Russians for the first ever, overall team gold medal.

Is there anyone alive who hasn't heard of the "Miracle on Ice"? Absolutely no one expected the 1980 U.S. Men's Olympic Hockey Team to win a medal, let alone the gold. The team, made up of amateur and collegiate players, beat the Russians in a 4-3 semi-final game. The crowd at Lake Placid, New York, went wild. The U.S. Men's Hockey Team went on to beat Finland in the gold medal game.

Continuing on the underdog theme, here's a big moment for a sport that doesn't always get the most attention at the Olympics: Greco-Roman Wrestling. American Rulon Gardner took on Russian Alexander Karelin at the 2000 games in Sydney; Karelin hadn't lost a wrestling match in 13 years. The match went into overtime, but in the end Gardner pulled off one of the greatest upsets in Olympic history.

Moving from the mat to the ice and figure skating, the list is long of special feats. Here are a few quick hits from spectacular performances.

When you think of Olympic figure skating, so much credit for its popularity has to go to the great Sonja Henie. The Norwegian won three gold medals in 1928, '32 and '36, more than any other ladies figure skater. Sonja Henie was an incredible athlete who excelled in other sports but focused on skating for the Olympics, along with a career as an actress. At one point she was one of the highest paid people in Hollywood. Truly revolutionary, she brought short skirts and style to the ice, and off the ice she was a powerful business woman who knew how to use her name.

Dorothy Hamill spurred a short bobbed haircut after she captured the nation's attention at the Olympics. Hamill won gold in 1976 at Innsbruck in Austria. One of her signature moves was a camel spin that turned into a sit spin on the ice, which became known as the "Hamill camel."

We can't talk about history and the Olympics without mentioning Jesse Owens. His skill, his poise, and his talent equaled none in Track and Field. As a black man, he was competing in Track and Field in 1936 in Berlin. Think of the times and being in Germany. Hitler's country saw Owens as an inferior athlete because of his skin color. He showed them, wining four gold medals: in the 100 meters, 200 meters, long jump, and 4x100 relay.

Lastly, the U.S. formed "the Dream Team" to

compete in Men's Hoops in 1992. This team was different as it included active NBA players: Michael Jordan, Magic Johnson, and Larry Bird. Nobody even got close to giving them a scare as they beat everyone by an average of 44 points. They beat Croatia in Barcelona for the Gold medal, and the crowd was crazed. People still talk about the Dream Team even with the U.S. fielding some incredible teams over the years. Then there was "the Redeem Team" that won gold medals in the 2008 and 2012 Summer Olympics, which included some of the biggest names of our era: LeBron James, Kobe Bryant, Carmello Anthony, and Chris Paul. Let's not forget who coached this team: the legendary coach of Duke, Mike Krzyzewski.

Imagine great locations, the best athletes in the World, and a ton of interesting competitions in both the summer and winter games. It's no surprise that so many of us have a trip to the Olympics on our bucket lists.

26

Iditarod

The Iditarod Trail Sled Dog Race has officially been around since 1973, although dog mushing was a way of life in Alaska from the late 1800s. Maybe even earlier, if you can imagine! It became a sport mostly because the mining towns were shutdown during the brutal winters. So there was no hauling of fur, food, gold ore, or any mining equipment that needed to be delivered.

The first race on record that paved the way for the current-day Iditarod Trail race happened in 1908 with The All-Alaska Sweepstakes. The dogsleds raced a total of 408 miles from Nome to Candle. The biggest thing to come out of this competition was the introduction of Siberian Huskies as a preferred racing dog in Alaska. Usually large-bred dogs like the Setter and the Alaskan Malamute were the dogs of choice before the Siberian became the king of the pack.

In writing this book, I was told by several Alaskans that I had to mention Balto, a dog who is immortalized with a statue in New York City's Central Park. You can also see this heroic dog stuffed and mounted in the Cleveland Natural History Museum. As the story goes, the race everyone still talks about is the 1925 Serum Run to Nome that wasn't for fun but to save the Eskimo children in Alaska who were in trouble. A diphtheria epidemic was threatening Nome; those kids had no immunity to the disease, with the nearest antitoxin in Anchorage. A batch of serum was sent to the town of Nenana by train, but that's as far as the engine could go.

Twenty mushers and 100 dogs had to relay the serum the rest of the way. To insure that the pack would make it, they ran in relays so that no dog would run over 100 miles of the 674 miles they needed to run to get to Nome. Gunnar Kassen, a Norwegian musher, and his trusty companion and lead dog, Balto, arrived in five and a half days. Most of the trip was through blinding snow and hurricane force winds. At one point, dogs and sled toppled, with the serum being buried in the snow. Kassen had to dig frantically and could barely see to find the stuff. Dog and man became legends after the trip. Even a short movie was produced: *Balto's Race to Nome*.

Thanks to Dorothy Page, years later the 1967 and 1969 Centennial Races led to the Iditarod race. It was held along portions of the trail and had money attached to it. Page sponsored the race to honor mushers. And with a purse of $25,000, it attracted 58 teams and was ultimately won by Isaac Okleasik. The race wouldn't have happened without the additional support of Joe Reddington, Sr., a musher himself who promoted the event and spread the word. Now he is often called, "the Father of Iditarod."

Those races, however, were very short—about 25 miles—and were nothing like the 1,049 mile race that is run today. The trail is made up of two routes: a northern route that is run on even-numbered years and a southern one that is run on odd-numbered years. Plenty has changed along the way, including checkpoints and starts for the race but not the harsh conditions. What an adventure as teams often race through blizzards and sub-zero temperatures across a rough landscape of frozen tundra, spruce forest hills, mountain passes and rivers.

Since 1983, the race has had a new tradition: a ceremonial start smack dab in the middle of downtown Anchorage. An auction is held where fans can bid to be a rider in a musher's sled from the starting line for the first 8 to 9 miles. This helps the mushers who finish outside of the top 20 spots and the prize money. The auction has become very popular and necessary to offset the expense for the teams that finish outside the money.

After that race, the dogs and mushers crash for the night before making their way to the real start of the race in Wasilla, Alaska, about 40 miles outside of Anchorage. Usually there are over 65 teams competing and not all are from Alaska. Mushers come from neighboring Canada, France, Norway, Austria, Italy, Sweden, and many other countries to test their mettle against the elements of the historic competition. The teams leave in ten-minute intervals, all with the same goal in mind—to hear the fire sirens when they cross the finish line first in Nome, and nab the $50,000 first prize.

The road to Nome is rough and dangerous, which is why 25 to 27 checkpoint stops are set up along the way. It depends on the musher's strategy as to when they will camp on the trail, but there are three mandatory stops: one 24-hour layover, one eight-hour layover along the Yukon River, and an eight-hour stop at White Mountain. Along the way the teams will pick up food, booties for the dogs, headlamps, sled parts, and whatever other equipment they brought with them and left in Anchorage. All of the packs are flown to the major stopping points so they can get supplies along the route.

Getting to the Iditarod is quite an accomplishment, as amateur mushers have to participate in three smaller races to qualify. To field a team, it can cost up to $40,000 to train, feed, house, and handle the dogs. Some of the professional people who compete run sled dog tours or write books and speak about their Iditarod experience to make a living. But you might be surprised to learn that many are surgeons, airline pilots, and even CEO's have been a part of the Iditarod competition.

Doug Swingley was the first musher outside of Alaska to win the Iditarod in 1995. He crossed the finish line in 9 days, 2 hours, 42 minutes, and 19 seconds. Since then the native Montanan has won three other times, just shy of five-time winner Rick Swenson. Swenson is considered an Alaskan, although he moved from Minnesota to compete in the Iditarod, his life-long dream. He ended up winning his first race at twenty-six years old, becoming the youngest person to ever win, and leading some to consider him the best of all time. The record for the fastest time goes to John Baker, who crossed into Nome in 8 days, 19 hours, and 46 minutes, claiming $50,000 and a new truck for finishing first in 2011.

As for the dogs, since the mid-1980s they have been examined by veterinarians before the start of the race and are tracked by microchip implants. On the trails, volunteer vets check everything from the dog's heart to its lungs and joints. A team is usually made up of 14 to 16 dogs, so that means there are about 900 to 1,000 in the race. These dogs are fast, averaging eight to twelve miles an hour, and are incredibly strong, weighing 75 pounds or more. Some are capable of pulling up to a half ton. Imagine what a whole team can do! In the end, the powerful lead dog of the winning team wins the golden harness and unlimited treats.

27

Snowboarding

Half-pipe, Boarder Cross, and Big Air are a few of the tricks of the trade that the best snowboarders in the world have mastered. It's not just the professionals who are tackling the mountains this way. Almost 8 million people around the world are going down runs on snowboards instead of using skis and poles.

So what is snowboarding? Think of surfing only on snow, and going down on a small board. The board is attached to the rider's feet with a boot hooked into a special binding, and without those poles, lots of balance is required. When snowboards first started to show up on the slopes in the late 1980s most were banned from ski areas. Less than 10 percent of ski slopes in the U.S. allowed snowboarding, and even then the rider would have to take a skills test to be allowed on the trails. Today almost every ski resort or park in North America and Europe allows and embraces snowboarding. Many have jumps, rails, and even some have half-pipes.

So how did this all start? One of the early pioneers was a guy named Tom Sims. He liked skateboarding so much he wanted to do it on the snow. He designed an early form of the board when he was just fourteen years old in the 1960s, by gluing carpet to a piece of wood and putting aluminum siding on the bottom. A decade later, he was selling them for a living. Credit should also be given to Sherman Poppen, who invented the Snurfer, very similar to a snowboard although instead of one board it was two skis. Poppen tied them together and attached a rope to one end so his daughter would have a little control careening down the hills. The idea took off and the rest is history as he sold his idea to a company that sold more than a million of them in a ten-year period.

Jake Burton Carpenter is also worth mentioning as a big fan of the Snurfer. When he was a kid he started trying to customize his own board. After finishing high school in New York, he scurried up to Vermont and began producing snowboards out of his garage for a living. Ultimately he founded Burton Boards in 1977—today a successful company that produces not just boards but also clothes and everything under the sun that goes along with snowboarding. A lot of the top names in snowboarding are sporting Burton Gear.

Fast forward to the 1998 Olympics in

Nagano, Japan and the whole world left out of the snowboarding craze was introduced to the sport. The men and women competed in two events: the giant slalom, similar to what you see on a downhill ski slope competition, and the half-pipe. What is the H.P.? The rider will go from side to side of a semi-circular ditch doing tricks along the way. The first ever gold medalist for snowboarding was Canada's Ross Rebagliati who won in the Giant Slalom.

As the popularity of the sport grew so did the interest in the superstars of the sport. The man everyone thinks of when you think of great feats on a snowboard is Shaun White, otherwise known as the "Flying Tomato," capturing attention around the globe with his daring feats. White won two gold medals his first 2006 Olympics in Torino, Italy and then again in 2010 at the Vancouver Olympics, both in the half-pipe. At the last Olympics, even though he knew he captured the gold, he did a second run that wowed the crowd. He pulled off his "Double McTwist 1260" move and scored 48.4 out of a possible 50 points.

There are so many Americans who are stars of this sport, including 24-year-old Hannah Teter. She won gold in the 2006 Olympics and silver in 2010. And like Shaun White, she transcends the sport. Teter posed for the 2010 Sports Illustrated swimsuit issue, and Ben and Jerry's named a limited edition "Maple Blondie" flavor after the girl from Vermont.

I had a conversation with Teter shortly after the last Olympics, and she was already talking about training hard for world competitions and dreaming about the next Olympics. She also goaded me into trying snowboarding but warned that butt pads are necessary for beginners.

28

Tour de France

The best professional bicyclists in the world spend three weeks in France competing for the final yellow jersey in arguably one of the most grueling sports in the world—the Tour de France. To make it on a team, there is no question that you have to be an elite rider, as the competition is stiff and riders come from all parts of the world.

The Tour is held each year in the beginning of July and features 200 bicyclists that race on teams of up to nine people. Typically, the race is 21-days long, covers 2,000 miles, and includes pedaling over two grueling mountain ranges—the Pyrenees and the Alps. Some breath-taking French towns, complete with centuries-old castles, are what the riders go past on most days. The route also will dip into neighboring countries like Italy, England, Denmark or Holland. The race alternates between clockwise and counter-clockwise routes and includes only two days rest. The riders are judged by time from the very start, so after every day or stage, the rankings are calculated. Imagine riding almost 100 miles every day!

An interesting tradition of the race is the daily awarding of different jerseys for the best riders in a couple of categories. The daily winner gets the yellow jersey; the green jersey goes to the sprints leader; a polka-dot jersey goes to the king of the mountains; and white to the best young rider under twenty-four years old. At the end of the day, a ceremony is held in the town where they finish, and the riders are awarded the jerseys along with a kiss from the models from Paris, who take the stage, as well. Rough, eh? The skill sets of the riders you see on the podium are different, and it makes sense since the stages range from flat, undulating, to mountainous.

Usually, the winner has won at least a stage or two, but there have been six exceptions to this rule, including in 2010 when Spain's Alberto Contador took the main prize. However, it is safe to say that the winner has usually mastered the mountains and the time trials. The trials are about 15 miles or less and feature a team trial and at least one or two individual ones. Team members help each other on the course, while the managers and mechanics also provide some support by following along in cars. The riders eat at feeding stages along the way, as well as carry fruit, sandwiches, energy bars, cokes, and other drinks packed in a bag that they grab so they can keep riding. Most riders take in up to 9,000 calories a day.

The first Tour took place in 1903 and was very different from today's race. Only 15 riders competed in the five stages that started and ended in Paris. Stages actually went through the night, finishing the next afternoon, and the race stretched from the end of May till July. Whoa! Quickly this was changed, and the race went from July 1st to the 19th and pay was included, amounting to 5 francs a day for some, with the winner getting six times the amount of money most working stiffs were making back in those times. Night racing was also dropped because of cheating as the judges had no idea if someone had gotten a ride.

You can't talk about the Tour de France, or cycling for that matter, and not mention Belgian Eddie Merckx. Turning pro in 1965, he won the World Championships 3 times, the Tour de France 5 times, and scores of other pro races. As an amateur, he won 80 races and was always a crowd favorite. In 1996, King Albert II of the Belgians bestowed the title of "Baron" to Merckx, However, as pleased as he was to receive the honor, it's still all about the bikes for the man considered to be the greatest cyclist of all time. Merckx can still be found in his bike factory tinkering and tweaking his line of bikes.

Here are some records from the Tour de France,

and believe me there are too many to mention in this book. American Lance Armstrong had won the most—seven consecutive times from 1999 to 2005. I'll explain in a minute. Armstrong became a national hero after winning his fight with testicular cancer well before his first win on the tour. When he was first diagnosed with the deadly disease, doctors told him he had a 20 percent chance to live and would never race again. He got experimental treatment from a facility in Indianapolis and beat the odds. Today you might see people wearing his yellow "Livestrong" rubber bracelets, a foundation that has raised hundreds of millions of dollars for cancer research.

However there was always a dark cloud following Armstrong, filled with innuendoes and flat out accusations that he was doping to win. In 2012, Cycling's governing body stripped Armstrong of his titles as well as other honors from 1999 to 2005 and banned him from cycling for life. They concluded, based on a report from the U.S. Anti-Doping Agency, that Armstrong and his team used performance enhancing drugs during those years, something he had always denied. That all changed in January of 2013, when he admitted in an exclusive interview with Oprah Winfrey that he used PED's throughout his career.

The other American to win is Greg Lemond, who did it in 1986, 1989, and 1990. Not surprisingly the country that has won it the most is France with 36, followed by Belgium riders that have captured the top spot 18 times. And the Spanish dominate as well with 13 wins.

Doping scandals have plagued the tour almost from the very beginning when riders were accused of consuming massive amounts of alcohol to dull the pain of the long mountain climbs. Lance Armstrong wasn't the only American stripped of his titles. Long before the fall of Armstrong, Floyd Landis was stripped of his Tour title. Landis won in 2006 after his epic comeback on Stage 17 of the race, making up 8 minutes overall for the win. Two weeks later the Phonak Cycling Team who Landis raced for announced that one of his urine samples tested positive for an unusually high ratio of testosterone to the hormone EPO, or epitestosterone. Almost a year later his title was taken away. Oscar Pereiro from Spain, who originally finished second, was declared the winner of the 2006 Tour.

Oh, and by the way, the other rider that had his title taken away was Frenchman Maurice Garin. He won in 1903 and wanted to repeat the feat the following year. In fact he was quoted as saying, "I'll win the Tour de France provided I'm not murdered before I get to Paris." He wasn't killed but was accused of taking a shortcut during the route by hopping on a train.

29

Mixed Martial Arts

Striking and grappling inside a giant cage, pitting one man against another, are broad descriptions of what is rapidly becoming one of the most popular sports in the world. Mixed Martial Arts, also known as Ultimate Fighting, allows a combination of full-combat, contact-sports moves. Think of boxing meets wrestling meets judo except the gloves are off.

Really its roots are very close to the Greco-Roman era in the early Olympics, where there was a combat sport known as Pankration. It used the boxing combinations with wrestling moves very close to what is now called MMA. If we jump ahead to the early 1970s, the idea of combining moves was really made popular by Bruce Lee. Only he called his philosophy "Jeet Kune Do." As he said many times during interviews, he thought the best fighter was the one who adapted to any style and formed their own individual style by not following a rigid system. If you watch any of his films you'll see that he lived this philosophy, grabbing a little of this and that which absolutely didn't fall into any definite discipline.

The UFC or Ultimate Fighting Championship made huge waves in the United States in 1993 when a Jiu-Jitsu fighter named Royce Gracie took out three challengers in less than six minutes. What? The pay-per-view UFC fights broke all kinds of records, rivaling professional wrestling and boxing in the pay-to-watch arena. The early days of the sport were thought to be kind of barbaric with rules that seemed to be all over the map. However, things would change to legitimize this new magic in a cage.

Now MMA has nine weight classes, from flyweight all the way up to super heavyweight, to help keep the fights fair and the fighters healthy. The bare fists have been replaced with small, open fingered gloves, and this keeps things moving where cuts were slowing things down in the past.

We all know about television timeouts in sports. Think the National Football League with any live event you have to be able to manipulate the time. So MMA added time limits to avoid long fights. Here's the way it usually goes: fights are three 5-minute rounds, and championship fights add two more rounds. There is also a stand-up rule where the referee can make the fighters jump up if he thinks they are resting on the ground much like the boxers "hug" in the ring.

As in any other sport one could argue all day long about the best fighters in the game, but in 2011 it's tough to argue against welter-weight champ Georges St. Pierre. He's won 22 of 24 mixed-martial-arts fights. And check out his belts: a black belt in Gaidojutsu and Brazilian Jiu-Jitsu, along with a 3rd dan black belt in Kyokushin karate. Saint-Pierre took up Kyokushin when he was seven to fight off a school bully. At one point in his life, the Canadian was a bouncer at a nightclub in Montreal. I bet he didn't have too many problems controlling someone who had a few drinks too many.

Retired mixed-martial-arts champ, Chuck Liddell, paved the way for guys like Saint-Pierre by helping to put the sport on the map back in the late 1990s. Liddell, a former wrestler at Cal Poly University, took out all contenders in 1998 and none bigger than kick boxer Guy Mezger. Liddell, who became the first UFC fighter to go and fight in the Pride Fighting Championships that year, knocked Mezger out cold in a fight people still talk about today.

I had a chance to talk with Mezger about that fight at Pride 14. He told me things looked good early on in the first round, slamming Liddell to the mat with a strike and a signature left kick to his face. Then as Mezger said, "I was stunned and out of it" within minutes of the second round. Mezger was no slouch with 42 wins out of 43 full-contact karate matches to his credit and 30 MMA victories.

We could write an entire book on Liddell, filled with his wild wins and antics. As far as records go in MMA, he won 21 of 29 matches, and his amateur kickboxing record was even better. He won 20 of 22 matches; 16 of those were knockouts. After retiring in December 2010, Liddell continues to train in San Luis Obispo, California, and he's put his business degree from Cal Poly to good use as the Vice President of UFC's business development.

PART ELEVEN

Rock Stars of Sports

30

Hot Shots: Past and Present

My list of hot shot athletes is in no particular order, just to head off any arguments ahead of time. Trust me, I've spent hundreds of hours on radio talking about the best of all time in sports across the board and it's hard to quantify. All sports have their unique challenges in different eras, being played with different rules, along with equipment changes through the years, and that's just scratching the surface.

I'm starting with Michael Jordan, as he transcended the game of basketball with his amazing dunks and ability to completely change a game. Here are his WOW numbers: Six championships in eight years, 32,292 points in his career. Only two other NBA players have scored more than MJ. He's number one in the record books with points per game, an average of 30, and he has two gold medals—one for his '82 appearance in Los Angeles and then a return trip to Barcelona in 1992 as part of the "Dream Team." That's not even the half of it! The bottom line is, who hasn't heard of this NBA Hall-of-Famer? He was the king of endorsements for a reason. Who doesn't own a pair of "Air Jordan" shoes?

"The Sultan of Swat," "the Bambino," or "the Babe" are just a few popular nicknames given to George Herman Ruth, maybe the best baseball player of all time. He certainly makes every sports fan's Top 10 list. Ruth started out as a pitcher for the Boston Red Sox and was traded to the Yankees, where he was promptly moved to right field and exploded at the plate. In a career that spanned from 1914 to 1935, the Babe was part of a New York Team that won seven pennants and four World Series. Ruth was the first player to ever hit 60 homers in a season; he did it in 1927. He ended his career with 714 home runs and .342 lifetime batting average—he was an amazing power hitter! Babe Ruth was one of the first players inducted into the Baseball Hall of Fame in 1939 and is credited with making baseball popular in the Roaring Twenties.

Muhammad Ali, known as Cassius Clay before he converted to Islam, was one of the best boxers in history and, like Ruth and Jordan, was more than an athlete; he was also a celebrity. Ali fought in 61 fights, winning 56 of them, and 37 were knockouts! So imagine that. Ali only lost five times in his heavyweight boxing career. Known for his trash-talking style, Ali had a way of intimidating opponents in and out of the ring. He described his style this way: "Float like a butterfly, sting like a bee." You could never count Ali out, and the one time everyone did was leading up to his fight with George Foreman, dubbed "The Rumble in the Jungle." The world was watching that bout in Kinshasa, Zaire, where Ali got his heavyweight crown back after dropping George Foreman in the eighth round. One of my favorite documentaries, *When We Were Kings,* really gives you a sense of how Ali dealt with the times and that fight.

In Track and Field, Jesse Owens was an athlete who seemingly took over the 1936 Olympics, winning four gold medals in Berlin, Germany. He won his medals in the 100 and 200 Meters, plus the 4x100 Meter Relay and the Long Jump competition. Before the Olympics, Owens had already set all kinds of records at Ohio State, where he was known as "the Buckeye Bullet." At one meet his Long Jump was measured at 26 feet, 8 ¼ inches. That high watermark wasn't broken until 1960.

In golf, Tiger Woods has won 14 of the Major professional golf tournaments, a close second to the record held by another great, Jack Nicklaus, with 18. Will Woods break his record? If he never wins another Major he still is one of the best of all time. He has more career PGA tour wins than any other active player with 71. Tiger's set all kinds of records, including being the youngest player ever to win a Grand Slam (all the Majors) and get to 50 wins on tour. He took a 20-week break in 2010 from the game after admitting to struggling with infidelity in his marriage to then wife Elin Nordegren. Back on tour, many of his competitors aren't counting Tiger out when it comes to winning more tournaments.

Tiger's friend, Roger Federer, also has a chance of making sports history by going down as the greatest tennis player of all time. Federer has shattered numerous records and is still actively on the tennis circuit in 2015. So far, he's won 17 Grand Slam titles and appeared in the finals of the slams more than any other player in the history of the sport more than 23-plus times. He has also won a record 5 ATP tour finals and, believe me, the list goes on and on.

As in other sports, there are countless hot shot Soccer stars I could mention, but I'll just tackle one for the purposes of this book. Topping my list is David Beckham. He started playing professional soccer at the age of 17 for Manchester United in 1992. He won the Premier League title six times, the Football Association Challenge Cup twice, and picked up many other trophies, including the La Liga Championship with Real Madrid in the final of his four seasons with that club.

A passing god, he was known for his bending

free kicks. When he signed with the LA Galaxy, an MLS Soccer team, in 2007, season tickets were gone within hours. FIFA named David Beckham one of the Top 100 best players of all time and he, like Michael Jordan and Tiger Woods, transcends his sport. His good looks and famous singer wife, Victoria Beckham, helped him earn huge endorsement dollars and, depending on the list, he is worth somewhere in the neighborhood of $350 million dollars.

Other old-school hot shots who make the list—some already mentioned in this book: Hank Aaron, Jackie Robinson, Carl Lewis, Joe Montana, Wilt Chamberlin, Kareem Abdul-Jabbar, Magic Johnson, Mario Lemieux, Pete Rose, Martina Navratilova, and Billie Jean King.

Current hot shots that make the list:

Tom Brady, Peyton Manning, Derek Jeter, Kobe Bryant, LeBron James, Rafael Nadal, and Serena and Venus Williams.

Final Invade the Man Cave Tip

Everyone likes to argue about what athlete, team or era is the best in sports, but it's all subjective. By now you are probably passionate about something or everything to do with sports, right? Either way, you have at least a little bit of knowledge to be dangerous and to INVADE THE MAN CAVE.

My next book will *Wow* you with Soccer
and sports of all sorts.